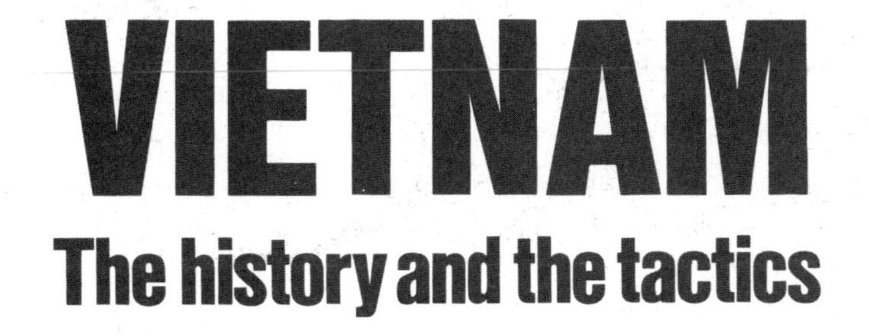
VIETNAM
The history and the tactics

Vietnam

The history and the tactics

Consultant editor John Pimlott

Crescent Books · New York

MICH

Consultant editor
John Pimlott is the author of a recently published book on the B-29 Superfortress and co-author of *Strategy and Tactics of War*. He has written a book on the Battle of the Bulge and has contributed to an encyclopedia of WorldWar II. He is Senior Lecturer in the Department of War Studies and International Affairs at Sandhurst.

The authors
Major F. A. Godfrey MC served in Malaya, Cyprus, Malta, Libya, Aden and Berlin before retiring from the British Army in 1969. He is a Senior Lecturer in the Department of War Studies and International Affairs at Sandhurst.

C. L. Cooper is a leading American authority on US foreign policy since World War II and is author of a number of books, including *The Lost Crusade*.

H. P. Willmott, Senior Lecturer in the Department of War Studies and International Affairs at Sandhurst, has a special interest in guerrilla warfare. He is the author of several books, among them *Pearl Harbor, A6M* and *B-17*.

John Kentleton is a lecturer in the School of History at the University of Liverpool. A visiting professor in American history at the University of Nevada, he specialises in modern American foreign policy.

A. D. Gilbert has contributed to a number of publications on military and naval subjects and his special areas of interest are World War II and civil-military relations post 1945.

Ian Beckett is a senior lecturer in the Department of War Studies and International Affairs at Sandhurst. He is the co-author of *Politicians and Defence*.

Acknowledgements
Photographs were supplied by ADN Zentralbild, API, Associated Press, Australian News and Information Bureau, René Dazy, Robert Hunt Library, Keystone, Popperfoto, Rex Features, Roger-Viollet, Sir Robert Thompson, US Airforce, US Army, US Marine Corps, US Navy, Viet Nam News Agency.

Editors Ashley Brown, Adrian Gilbert
Designer Dave Johnson

This 1982 edition is published by Crescent Books, distributed by Crown Publishers, Inc
a b c d e f
Printed in Italy by Sagdos SpA

Library of Congress Cataloging in Publication Data
Main entry under title:

Vietnam, the history and the tactics.

1. Vietnamese Conflict, 1961-1975. 2. Indo-chinese War, 1946-1954.
DS557.7.V563 1982 959.704 82-12724
ISBN 0-517-39375-1

Contents

Introduction

The Indochinese Peninsula, now comprising the states of Vietnam, Kampuchea (Cambodia) and Laos, has been the scene of almost continuous conflict since 1945. The scale of that conflict may have fluctuated according to the degree of outside involvement, but the sad fact remains that for nearly 40 years the indigenous population has not experienced settled peace. Wars which began as anti-colonial, nationalist struggles quickly developed into confrontation between the rival ideologies of western democracy and communism and, since the victory of the latter in 1975, have degenerated into internecine bids for local supremacy. Literally millions of people – among them Vietnamese, Khmers, Laotians, Montagnards, French, American and Chinese – have been killed or injured and there are no signs that the tally is yet complete.

This is tragic enough, but the political consequences of the violence have been no less traumatic. At a local level, national boundaries have been redrawn, the enforcement of political change has meant widespread repression and entire populations have been forcibly moved. Economies have suffered from the decades of destruction, social development has been retarded and an enormous refugee problem has virtually defied solution. What was once a beautiful and potentially self-sufficient area has been transformed by war into a ravaged land, areas of which will take generations to recover. In addition, the spread of communism has drawn the region into the whirl of Sino-Soviet rivalry, with both great powers seemingly intent upon achieving control through their chosen allies. It all makes the future look bleak for the local population.

The world watches

But the ramifications are even wider, for the victory of communism, regardless of continuing arguments about the form to be finally adopted, has deeply affected the western world. France and America, two of the most powerful representatives of the democratic system, were defeated in Indochina, despite their enormous military and economic resources. This called into question the resolve and effectiveness of democratic nations faced with the steady, determined spread of a rival ideology and produced a significant undermining of national confidence in the very processes of democracy. In the case of France this was manifested not only in a lack of public support for the war in Indochina between 1945 and 1954 but also in a hardening of military attitudes which was to lead eventually to attempted coups and political chaos as apparently similar problems were experienced in Algeria (1954-62).

Admittedly the reaction in America was not so extreme, but the consequences of her involvement in Indochina from 1965 to 1973 were, if anything, even more damaging. As the American armed forces, despite growing numerical strength and almost unlimited technological expertise, failed to destroy the threat to South Vietnam, domestic opinion began seriously to question the validity of the war effort, particularly as casualty rates rose for no tangible results. Such soul-searching was undoubtedly exploited by clever communist propaganda which managed to portray the United States as a neo-colonialist bully, denying the rights of self-determination to the peace-loving peoples of Indochina, but there was more to it than that. Democracy is always subject to internal criticism – after all, freedom of expression is a fundamental part of the democratic system – and public opinion can affect government decisions, weakening the resolve of the state to stand firm against a threat. When that threat is not obvious or immediate – and who in America could really fear the spread of communism in South-east Asia? – casualties and costs become difficult to justify. The government, short of imposing the war effort upon the people (an action which would in itself be a negation of democratic principles), is left with impossible options. If the government weakens the war effort, it will probably lose the war; if it strengthens it, public support and more importantly perhaps, their votes, will disappear. The Vietnam War was to see this dilemma destroy President Johnson and contribute to the premature retirement of his successor: the long-term ramifications, characterised by the painful process of an American recovery of confidence, are still with us today. They affect not only the United States but the whole of the western world.

It would be wrong to imagine, however, that the violence of the last four decades represents a unique chapter in Indochinese history, for the region, by virtue of its strategic position as a link between the cultures of India and China, has had more than its share of rivalry and conflict. As early as 207 BC the area around what is now Hanoi, on the Red River Delta, was conquered by a rebel Chinese warlord, Trieu Da, who created his own kingdom stretching into the southern provinces of China. Such independence of action did not last, being forcibly ended in 111 BC by the Han Emperor Wu Ti, Although this marked the beginning of a Chinese suzerainty over northern Vietnam which was to last for a thousand years, it did not mean an end to the violence. Local resistance to Chinese rule developed, only to be ruthlessly repressed, and wars were fought against the Indian-orientated states of Indochina – Champa in the south and Funan to the west. By the 10th century, with the Chinese Tang Dynasty in decline, a measure of autonomy was gained for northern Vietnam, but this merely presaged a further 400 years of intermittent war as successive Mongol and Chinese invasions were defeated, the last by Le Thai To in 1427.

The Le Dynasty remained in nominal control until as late as 1786, although from about 1600 rivalries grew between the Trinh and Nguyen factions within the state. Nevertheless, during this period Champa was conquered (1471) and the fertile Mekong Delta was wrested from the Khmer regime in Cambodia (1760). Independent Vietnam was territorially at its height.

French conquest

This strength was illusory, however. Civil war broke out in the last decades of the 18th century, with the major contenders the Nguyen faction in the south and the Ray Son brothers in the north. Peace did not return until 1802 when the Nguyen Emperor Gia Long took Hué and Hanoi. He was never a fully independent ruler, however, for he could only maintain his power through mercenaries raised by the French missionary Pigneau de Behaine, an early representative of the western state most interested in the region. At this stage official French involvement was minimal, but when Gia Long and his successor, Tu Duc, began to react against such outside interference, chiefly by instigating policies of anti-Catholicism, the Paris authorities were inexorably drawn in to protect their people.

In 1847 the port of Danang was bombarded by a French fleet and ten years later, as Tu Duc showed no signs of relenting, a major Franco-Spanish assault was mounted against the north. The campaign was by no means a walkover (in 1862 the Spanish withdrew because of the high costs) but by 1863 Tu Duc had been forced to cede his southern provinces, around Saigon, to France and to open his northern ports to western trade. This merely allowed the French to tighten their grip, extending their rule over the whole of what became known as Cochin China. At much the same time Cambodia, under increasing pressure from both Vietnam and Thailand, signed a Protectorate Treaty with France. The empire – to be known as the *Union Indo-Chinoise* – was completed between 1883 and 1893 as central Vietnam (Annam) and northern Vietnam (Tongking or Tonkin) were taken by force and Laos became a protectorate.

Colonial exploitation

The French found themselves in possession of a huge area, potentially ripe for commercial exploitation but immensely difficult to control. With the exception of the two Vietnamese delta regions, around Saigon and Hanoi, and a long thin coastal plain, the land was rugged and inhospitable, comprising mountain chains, swamps and virtually inaccessible plateaus. The climate was governed by the annual monsoon (May to September) and although this helped the area to produce vast quantities of rice, it made most other commercial enterprises difficult. Communications were poor or non-existent and the region as a whole was less than homogeneous. Chinese-orientated northeners would not co-operate with the more Indianised southeners, no love was lost between Vietnamese and Khmers and a host of minority mountain tribes (known to the French as Montagnards) were distrusted by all. To make matters worse, some areas retained their own nominal rulers – as was the case with Annam, Cambodia and Laos – while others were no more than colonies under direct French administration. It was a confused package of control, fraught with potential crises.

Divide and rule

In the event the French protected their presence through a combination of strong military action and astute political juggling, suppressing all signs of resistance and playing one ethnic group off against another. It worked surprisingly well between the 1890s and 1940s, chiefly because the opposition which did exist was fragmentary and weak. Nationalists such as Phan Boi Chau tried to raise rebellion both before and during World War I but their appeal tended to be limited to specific ethnic aspirations and they were easily contained.

What was needed was a unifying cause capable of drawing together and exploiting all aspects of Indochinese nationalism and this did not begin to emerge until the 1920s, when the new ideals of communism spread from Russia. Even then, nationalist rivalries precluded immediate success and it was not until the Vietnamese Nationalist Party of Nguyen Thai Hoc had been suppressed by the French after the abortive Yen Bay uprising of February 1930 that the communists could begin to organise an effective structure. Nguyen ai Quoc, the Annamese leader of the Revolutionary League of the Youth of Vietnam who became better known as Ho Chi Minh, founded the Indochinese Communist Party while in exile in Hong Kong in 1930, but a series of failed risings the following year showed that his appeal was not as broad as the title of his organisation implied. Ho remained in exile, travelling to China to receive advice and training from Mao Tse-tung's communist forces, and waited for the right moment for revolt. It was not long in coming.

French rule in Indochina was seriously undermined in June 1940, when Metropolitan France fell to the Germans, for although the Hanoi administrators did not hesitate to support the new government at Vichy, they were effectively isolated and vulnerable to external pressure. Thus, when Japan, already at war with China and intent upon further expansion, started to make demands, there was little that could be done to deny them. In September 1940 the Vichy authorities in Indochina agreed to close the supply route between Haiphong and southern China and gave permission for Japanese forces to use airfields and bases in Vietnam. It was a fatal error, destroying the myth of French invincibility and tying Hanoi inextricably to Japanese policies.

This was exactly what Ho Chi Minh had been waiting for. In 1941 he used it to draw together the disparate strands of nationalism and communism, at least in Vietnam, founding the League for the Independence of Vietnam (*Doc Lap Dong Minh Hoi*, or Viet Minh). Despite attempts by the Nationalist Chinese to prevent this – they arrested Ho and kept him in prison for nearly a year – the need to put pressure on Japan took precedence. By 1943 Ho had joined General Vo Nguyen Giap in the mountains of Tonkin and active resistance had begun.

Viet Minh strategy was based upon Mao Tse-tung's concept of 'revolutionary war,' for although the ostensible purpose was to oppose the Vichy French and Japanese, there can be little doubt that the ultimate aim was always political power. Revolutionary war envisages a campaign divided into three interlocking phases, geared to the capabilities of its practitioners. In the first phase time is spent in political preparation of the peasant masses, creating 'safe bases' in remote areas which will sustain the revolution as it develops. Once in existence, these bases require protection and need to expand. Given the small scale of revolutionary activity at this stage, the only method available is guerrilla warfare, exploiting the local knowledge and political resolve of the people.

Disintegration of the state

The second phase entails ambushes, hit-and-run attacks and selected raids against isolated enemy outposts, each of which should produce captured weapons and provide invaluable military experience. Gradually the enemy will be forced to spread his army out and, as the guerrillas grow stronger, will cease to protect the political centres of the state. This allows the revolutionaries to enter the third and final phase – that of open battle against a weakened enemy force, leading to the usurpation of political power.

Filling a vacuum

In the event the Viet Minh approached victory in 1945 without having to go this far. Receiving military equipment from the Americans, they waged an increasingly effective guerrilla campaign but did little to produce the 'revolutionary moment'. That was done for them, initially by the Japanese takeover of Indochina in March 1945, which conveniently rid the area of French forces, and then by the sudden Japanese surrender five months later, which left a political vacuum in Indochina. This the Viet Minh sought to fill, proclaiming an independent Democratic Republic of Vietnam in Hanoi on 2 September and looking to the Americans to prevent a French return. But the French were determined to reassert their authority in Vietnam; and were, therefore, on an inevitable collision course with the equally determined forces of Viet Minh.

JOHN PIMLOTT

1. The French War

Peace came to most of the world in 1945,
but not to Vietnam. The former colonial regime
of the French had been discredited and humiliated by the
Japanese, and nationalist feelings ran high. As the French tried to
re-establish themselves they met stiff opposition, from the communist-dominated
Viet Minh, and although the European power did take over the cities, it found
itself unable to control the countryside. For European colonialism was now
confronted by the disciplined cadres of a communist revolutionary army,
determined to stop at nothing to achieve its goals. At the head of this
force were brilliant, ruthless men, who for ten years waged an
unrelenting guerrilla struggle, waiting for the French to weaken
or overstretch themselves. And finally, in the remote village
of Dien Bien Phu, came their opportunity.

*Hardened French paratroops take a break from the fighting.
Although France deployed some of her best troops in Indochina – including the
paratroops and Foreign Legion – victory went, ultimately,
to the Viet Minh.*

Postwar Indochina

Left: Postwar Indochina, the land to which French administration returned in 1945. The re-assertion of control by the French was strongly resisted by nationalists in all areas, but especially in the three areas of Vietnam – Cochin China in the south, Annam in the centre and Tonkin in the north. In Cochin China and Annam, communist guerrillas waged a low-level campaign, but in Tonkin the insurgents established strong bases in the mountains of the Viet Bac, and fought a more intensive campaign. Below: Ho Chi Minh, the man whose inspired, ruthless and dedicated leadership saw the communists to victory. He set up the coalition of nationalists that became known as the Viet Minh, and soon brought it under communist domination.

The French return to Indochina after World War II was beset with problems: a number of factors which, though not related, interacted to confront them with the gravest difficulties as they moved to re-establish their authority in the area.

In the first place, the collapse of the Europeans in the face of Japanese expansion during World War II had raised questions as to their invincibility in the minds of Asian peoples and led in turn to a rise in nationalist aspirations, at least among the politically motivated and educated. Nowhere was this more apparent than in Indochina. Communism was also developing into a vigorous force following the victory of the Soviet Union in the war in Europe and the increasing influence of Mao Tse-tung, so soon to be victorious in China. In Indochina itself Ho Chi Minh, a determined and skilful leader, welded the forces of nationalism and communism together and made of them a major threat to French ambitions.

The French task was made still more difficult by the attitude of the government of the United States which, ever mindful of its own past, made it quite clear that in its view the European colonial territories in the Far East should move rapidly towards independence. Concerning Indochina President Roosevelt, as early as 1943, had let it be known that he did not want France to return there after the war.

Filling the vacuum

These factors created difficulties enough but of perhaps even greater significance was the French experience in World War II. The collapse of France following the German attack in 1940 led to divisions right through French society, between those who supported the Vichy government and others who rallied to de Gaulle's call to join the Free French movement. These differences persisted even after the establishment of de Gaulle's government in Paris in 1944 and they did much to inhibit the formulation of clear, decisive foreign and colonial policy. In addition, French resources were so limited that France was unable to return to her possessions in the Far East soon enough and in sufficient strength to assert her authority in the wake of the sudden Japanese surrender in August 1945. There was in Indochina a political and military vacuum which was too long in being filled and this gave the opponents of France an opportunity which they swiftly seized.

At the last of the major Allied wartime conferences, held at Potsdam in July-August 1945, it was agreed that Indochina should be occupied, following the Japanese surrender, by two forces: in the north by those of Chiang Kai-shek's Nationalist Chinese Army and in the south by formations of the Allied Commander in South-east Asia. This tidy arrangement was, however, forestalled by the earlier involvement of the two forces which were ultimately to be in contention for control of the whole territory: the grouping of nationalist and communist parties in Vietnam known as the Viet Minh, and the French government itself.

The Japanese had, throughout the war, allowed the Vichy government in Indochina to continue to function but after de Gaulle's government in France came into being they were quick to recognize the likely dangers to their own position and they ordered the French to place themselves under Japanese authority. The move was resisted by some French military units but after bloody fighting in several areas the Japanese achieved their aim. With the situation militarily under control the Japanese pressured Bao Dai, the Emperor of Annam, to announce the independence of Vietnam. This he did with some reluctance on 11 March 1945.

Bao Dai's authority was, however, minimal as the Viet Minh was already organized and in control of large areas of Tonkin (often spelt Tongking) in the north of Vietnam. On 2 September 1945, the day the Japanese formally surrendered, Ho Chi Minh, Secretary-General of the Viet Minh, proclaimed the establishment of the Democratic Republic of Vietnam. Having in vain sought recognition of Vietnamese independence from the French, Bao Dai abdicated in favour of Ho Chi Minh's provisional government, calling as he did so on the people of Vietnam to support the new republic.

Above: The Emperor Bao Dai, puppet ruler of Annam, on his throne in 1938 just before the train of events which transformed his position. Bao Dai was a shadowy figure, who had been manipulated by various forces and interests – the French, the Japanese and Vietnamese nationalists – but he was himself a wily, scheming politician. Right: A communist poster celebrating the event that gave the Viet Minh their greatest hope: Mao Tse-tung's triumph in China.

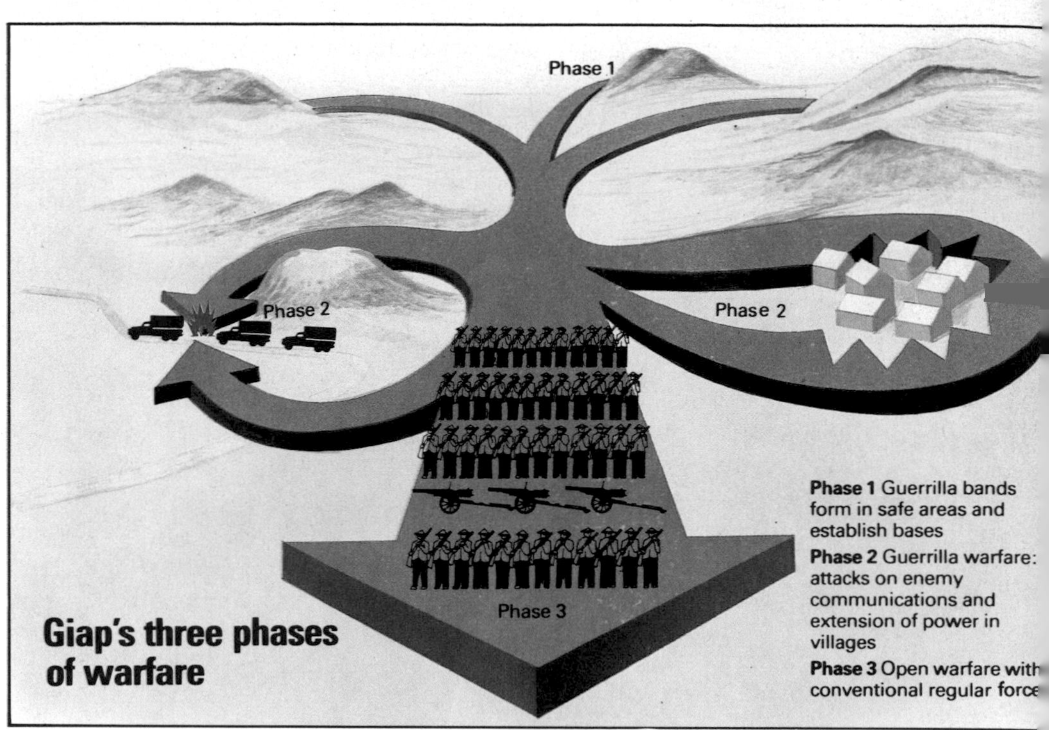

Above right: Revolutionary warfare was the method chosen by the Viet Minh as the best route to their goal of an independent communist Vietnam. Based upon the theories and practice of Mao Tse-tung, revolutionary warfare was, in essence, a means of converting ones weaknesses into strengths. Small forces could secure a strong base in a remote area; could then gradually extend their control over the population and attack enemy weak spots; finally, sufficient forces could be gathered to meet the enemy in open battle.
Above: The men who imposed revolutionary warfare – the directors of the Viet Minh war effort, including Ho Chi Minh (second from left) and Vo Nguyen Giap (standing).
Opposite below: The actual military tactics of the Viet Minh were like those of all guerrilla armies. The ambush was a classic manoeuvre. A French convoy (A) would be stopped and forced to seek cover by a combination of mines (B) and small arms fire (C). The mortars and light artillery (D) could be brought to bear on static targets until the coup de grâce *was administered by waves of infantry. Opposite above: The most effective weapons in guerrilla warfare were those that gave small groups of infantry maximum fire power: light machine guns, sub-machine guns and rifle-launched grenades or light mortars.*

Conflict in Tonkin

The first representatives of de Gaulle's government arrived in Vietnam by parachute on 23 August 1945. They were two Commissioners, one of whom landed in Hanoi and one in Saigon, and they were charged with the task of re-establishing French authority in Vietnam. To this end they enlisted the support of those members of the former Vichy Indochinese administration sympathetic to the Gaullist cause.

Early in September British forces arrived in Saigon in accordance with the Potsdam agreement and by the end of the month, with British help, French authority was restored in Saigon, the capital of Cochin-China (southern Vietnam). By January 1946 the French were loosely in control throughout Cochin-China. The comparative ease with which this was accomplished was in part explained by the weakness of the Viet Minh organization in the south.

But Tonkin in the north was a different matter. The Nationalist Chinese forces, which arrived in September 1945, established a reasonably friendly relationship with Ho Chi Minh's government based in Hanoi. Ho fostered this relationship by deliberately stressing the nationalist aspirations of the Viet Minh. In contrast, the Chinese behaved in a hostile manner to the nascent French administration in Hanoi and did all they could to hinder French efforts to regain control in the northern part of the country.

There ensued a period of several months in which negotiations took place between the French and the Chinese on one hand and the French and the Viet Minh on the other. The upshot of these discussions was that the Chinese were to withdraw from Vietnam in June 1946 consequent upon the French agreeing to relinquish all rights over concessions long held in China itself. As for Ho Chi Minh, he accepted an agreement with the French, signed on 6 March 1946, which gave to the Vietnamese Republic internal freedom with its own government and armed forces as part of an Indochinese federation incorporated into the French Union, a Gaullist organization meant to sustain French cultural and economic interests in former colonial possessions. For her part France agreed to withdraw all her own armed forces over a five-year period.

On the day this agreement was signed French naval forces arrived off Haiphong in the Bay of Tonkin. The French fleet was resisted by the local Nationalist Chinese commander who claimed he did not know of the agreement between the French and Ho Chi Minh. There ensued a heavy naval bombardment following

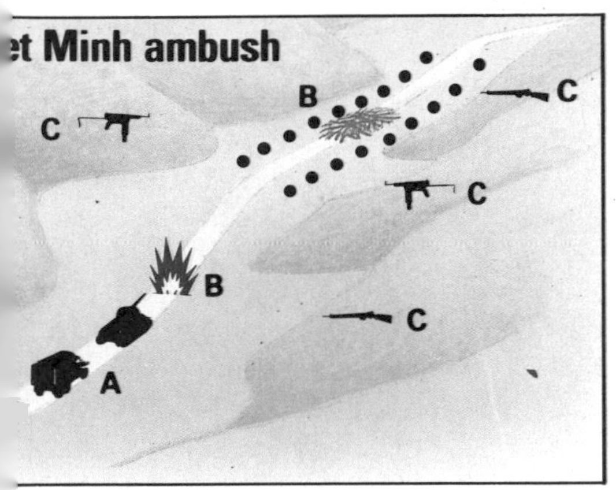

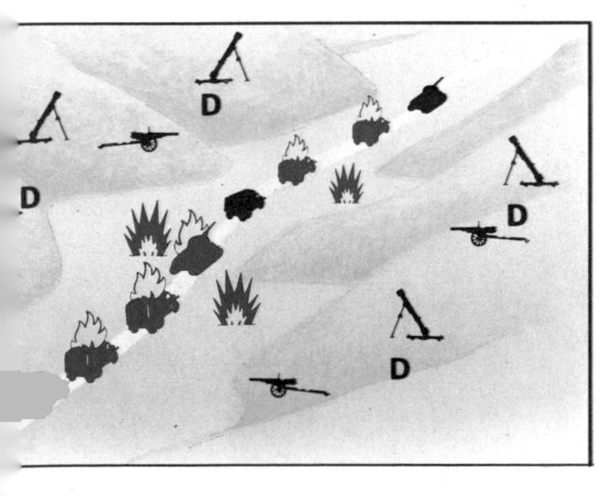

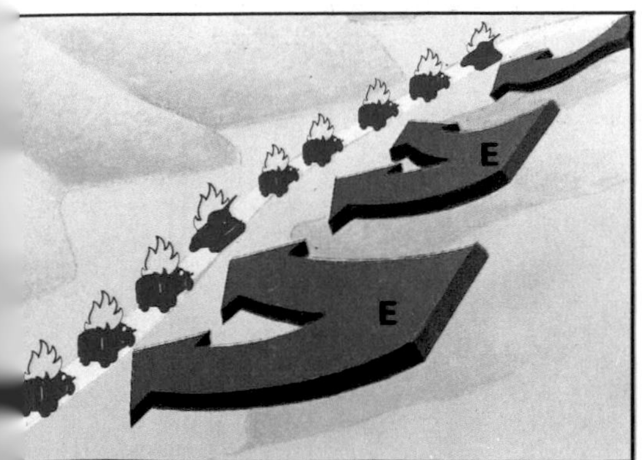

which the French forces landed at Haiphong and moved quickly to establish themselves in Hanoi. Thus they eventually secured a military presence in the north of Vietnam.

With French authority now re-established, albeit loosely, throughout Indochina it now remained to be seen whether French political objectives could be achieved in their further dealings with the Viet Minh and whether, if they were not, the French were capable of imposing a military solution on the peoples of Vietnam, Cambodia and Laos.

The war begins

Throughout the summer of 1946 an uneasy cooperation continued between the Viet Minh and the French. Confidence was eroded on both sides largely because neither side spoke with one voice. Statements emanating from French authorities in Saigon and Hanoi were conflicting and there was no firm lead coming from Paris as the French government was inactive during the drawing-up and adoption of the new constitution. The Viet Minh for its part exacerbated the situation by approving its own constitution which made no mention of an Indochinese federation nor of membership of the French Union.

Meanwhile the strength of the French garrison was increased until it was capable of maintaining strongpoints in most of the towns of Indochina. The Viet Minh forces under the leadership of Vo Nguyen Giap was deployed in Hanoi with many units based in rugged, inaccessible country to the north of the city towards the Chinese frontier. It too was increased in size and organized into regular and militia units, ever better armed and equipped, as supplies found their way into Tonkin from sympathizers across the Chinese frontier.

In November and December 1946 a number of incidents in Haiphong and Hanoi raised the level of tension to breaking point and, despite attempts by Ho Chi Minh and senior French officials to calm the situation down, war became inevitable.

At the outset of hostilities the French military command was confident that it could quickly bring the situation under control and pacify the whole of Indochina. It assumed that it was about to undertake a colonial war and its strategy was geared to holding key points throughout the country and at the same time making available mobile forces whose task was to seek out and destroy the enemy leadership and main formations. Whereas such a strategy had proved effective in colonial campaigns before World War II, especially in North Africa,

it was to fail in Indochina for two reasons. In the first place the terrain and vegetation in Indochina was a far cry from the open landscape of North Africa, and the French quickly found that a few isolated pickets were insufficient to protect roads between their garrisons. They never had large numbers of troops to spare to guard their lines of communication between key points. Secondly, they did not bargain for the revolutionary war fought by the Viet Minh. The French were the first Europeans to experience this phenomenon, developed and adapted from the experiences of Mao Tse-tung in China in the thirties. They had no reason to know, for example, that the loss of senior commanders by the Viet Minh was unlikely to affect the capacity of its armies to function, or that the Viet Minh forces would normally be scattered throughout the land in 'penny packets', only being concentrated briefly for a particular operation, thereby minimizing the opportunity for surprise attack by the French.

The initial reaction of the Viet Minh on the outbreak of hostilities was to withdraw their regular units into the remote and difficult areas of the Viet Bac (the region of Tonkin between Hanoi and the Chinese border). At the same time locally raised units of militia attempted to cut the French lines of communication and assault some French garrisons. French determination aided by their massive superiority in firepower led to failure of this general uprising and the Viet Minh disappeared from view. For the next three years they remained almost inactive militarily and concentrated on building up their strength by recruiting, training and equipping their army, by developing their supply system and above all by working to persuade the people of Indochina to rally to their cause.

French dilemma

In 1947 the French committed a large part of their limited forces in a major operation lasting some five months in which they attempted to strike at the main command elements of the Viet Minh and to bring their regular forces to battle. While they achieved some local successes they failed in both objectives and, even more importantly, by weakening their garrisons in other areas in order to concentrate sufficient troops for this operation they allowed the Viet Minh to spread their influence further afield unimpeded. This latter problem was one faced by the French forces right through the campaign until 1954, and it could only ever have been resolved by additional troops being made available to the commander-in-chief by the French government.

In 1948 the French carried out few offensive operations and spent the year building up their strength in the Red River Delta around Hanoi and Haiphong.

Top: Naval strength had been essential to the successful re-establishment of the colonial regime. Above: French armour meant that the Viet Minh could not hope to compete in open battle over great stretches of the countryside. Right: Moroccan tirailleurs during a sweep through a village in 1951. Opposite below: Vietnamese infantry, supported by French tanks, during Operation Brochet, *another sweep through the countryside. Opposite far right: By 1949, the Viet Minh controlled large areas of Vietnam leaving the French in a vulnerable position on the Cao Bang-Lang Son ridge. Opposite right: A French machine-gun team mans an outpost near Dien Bien Phu.*

In the south they reinforced their position in Cochin-China generally and in this they received some help from Vietnamese groups hostile to the Viet Minh cause.

By the end of 1949 the Viet Minh had to a large degree perfected their organization and, further, had had their position greatly strengthened by Mao Tse-tung's success in China. Now Chinese territory, beyond the threat of French action, could be used as a sanctuary for storing supplies and for training. Weapons and other equipment would reach the Viet Minh from Chinese sources in ever-growing quantities. The French were aware of this likely adverse effect on their own position and decided to withdraw their garrisons from remoter areas to the north of Hanoi except where there were particularly important key points. This plan was meant to allow them to strengthen their forces in the Red River Delta, the major rice-growing area of Tonkin, and deny essential food to the Viet Minh.

Viet Minh zones 1949

Right: The defeat of the French along the Cao Bang–Lang Son ridge in 1950 was the most obvious sign that they could not come to grips with the strategy of the Viet Minh. After mounting pressure, Dong Khe fell to the communists, and all attempts to retrieve the situation met with failure.
Below: The events of 1950 certainly did much to boost Viet Minh morale and to weaken that of the French; but they also had a very clear strategic importance. The easiest way to supply the Vietnamese insurgents from now-communist China was through Cao Bang and Lang Son from the rail-head at Nanning; and henceforth Viet Minh stockpiles of armaments would continue to grow.

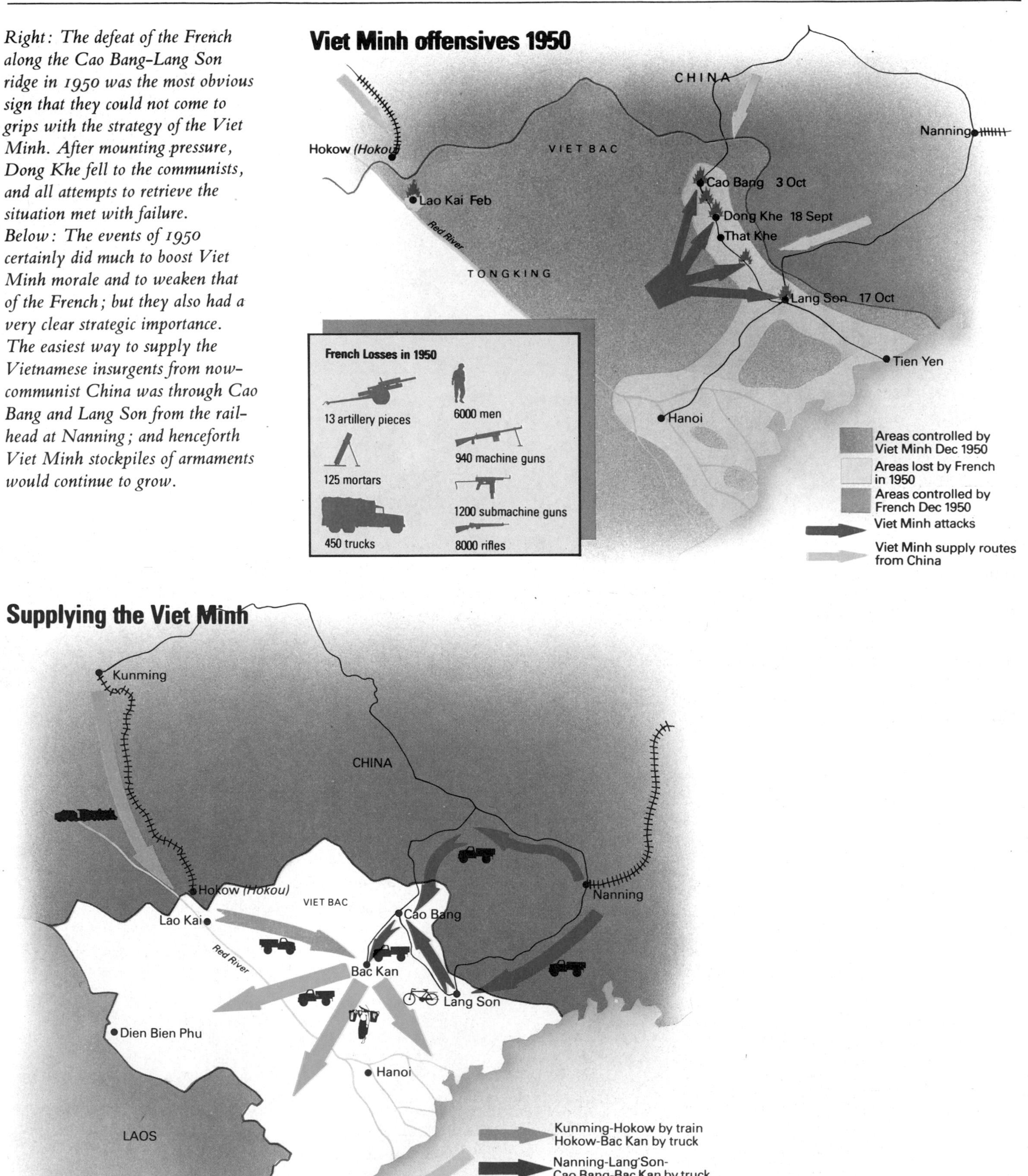

The plan was recommended by General Revers, the French Army Chief of Staff, who made a brief visit to Indochina in May 1949. The reasoning behind the plan was sensible enough, recognizing the futility of attempting to hold on to remote outposts of little strategic value. It would also allow for the creation of further mobile reserves capable of reacting to Viet Minh attacks in more important areas. Unfortunately the plan was 'leaked' to the Viet Minh who made much propaganda value of it, highlighting the apparent French weakness and inability to resist Viet Minh pressure.

The French withdrawal took place nevertheless, and was accompanied by the first really aggressive Viet Minh operations. Between late 1949 and April 1950 a series of offensives was launched against French strongpoints which culminated in the Viet Minh gaining control of the whole of Tonkin to the north and east of Hanoi save for a string of posts running north from the Gulf of Tonkin along the 'Route Coloniale 4' (RC4) to Cao Bang, a garrisoned town in the very north-eastern corner of Tonkin close to the border with Red China.

Communist gains

Throughout the summer of 1950 the Viet Minh concentrated their forces on RC4 and in attack after attack they captured one or other of the small towns on the road only to be driven out again by French counter-attacks. Both sides suffered heavy casualties as the French fought valiantly to keep the road open and the Viet Minh just as determinedly to cut off Cao Bang. The latter were given a big boost when in August at the height of the fighting the French government decided to reduce its forces in Indochina by 9000 men and forbade the use of conscripts in the region.

In September the Viet Minh mounted a major assault against Dong Khe, a town part way along RC4. On this occasion they were successful and thus cut off Cao Bang and other French garrisons to the north of the town. The French Commander-in-chief acted immediately. He dispatched a task force of 3500 Moroccan troops to retake Dong Khe so that the beleaguered garrison at Cao Bang could extricate itself along RC4. He ordered the commander at Cao Bang to destroy all his heavy weapons and equipment and march on foot southwards through Dong Khe. The Cao Bang commander decided to ignore the order to destroy his vehicles and guns and instead of making use of the comparative safety of foot tracks he drove southwards along RC4 through ambush after ambush set up at little cost by the Viet Minh. The remnants of the garrison eventually reached the foothills overlooking Dong Khe where they joined up with the remaining elements of the Moroccan troops who had been unable to hold on to the town. Despite a last-minute parachute drop of three battalions the situation could not be retrieved and those left alive were either killed or captured in a final ferocious attack by triumphant Viet Minh troops. In this abortive series of operations the French lost some 6000 men and enough weapons and equipment to supply a whole Viet Minh division. For France it was the biggest colonial military defeat to date, while the Viet Minh had succeeded in seizing virtually the whole of Tonkin north of Hanoi: a major victory.

As a result of this disastrous setback French morale plummeted and in a desperate attempt to retrieve the situation General Jean de Lattre de Tassigny was appointed High Commissioner and Commander-in-Chief of the Army in Indochina in December 1950. He came with a great reputation behind him as a military leader in World War II. He was a

Above top: The Viet Minh used a variety of methods to supply troops in the field, and bicycles were one of the most effective. With large gangs of porters, heavy loads could be split up and transported, and the bicycle had the advantage that it could be pushed over ground impassable for trucks. Above: While the Viet Minh supply network became more and more efficient, the French faced a constant drain of their resources as their communications were harried at every point, and road transport became liable to ambush. Here, an armoured car lies victim to the Viet Minh.

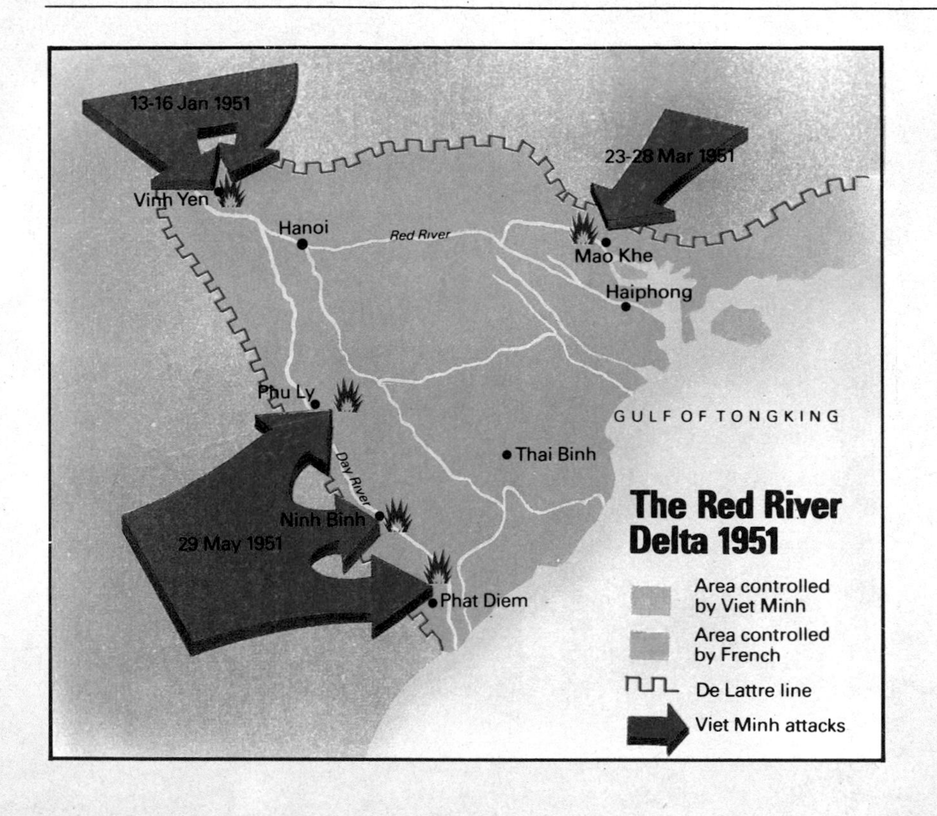

man of strong personality, a certain extravagance of style and imbued with a dogged determination to achieve results: his combination of civil and military authority provided him with the power to do so. In his first statement on arrival he offered no easy victory and no hope of reinforcements but he gave the French Expeditionary Force what they really needed at that juncture: decisive leadership.

The fight for the Delta

Among the measures introduced by de Lattre after arrival was the construction of a series of fortified posts in the Red River Delta providing protection for Hanoi – the 'de Lattre' line. Whatever happened in the outlying regions he was determined that Hanoi would be defended. He also devoted much attention to the encouragement of young Vietnamese to fight side by side with the French against the communists.

Within a few weeks of de Lattre's arrival General Giap, no doubt encouraged by his successes of the previous autumn and sensing that the French will was faltering, decided on a major gamble with the intention of seizing Hanoi. Between January and June 1951 he launched three large-scale attacks: two in the Red River Delta west of Hanoi and one directed against the port of Haiphong. He used no less than five different divisions for this assault but his men were for the most part inexperienced and the French, though heavily outnumbered, succeeded in beating off the enemy. Their superior firepower cut down the massed infantry attacks as Viet Minh troops approached their positions. The casualties on the Viet Minh side were horrifying: in one action alone, lasting only five days, they suffered 6000 men killed. The French success seemed to confirm the value of the Revers plan and de Lattre pressed ahead with the construction of his defensive belt round Hanoi.

This costly failure led the Viet Minh to retreat from the idea of conventional attacks and they returned to the use of guerrilla methods of warfare. Instead of going in strength for the wide-open lowlands of the Delta area they turned their attention to the interior mountainous regions where the French forces found

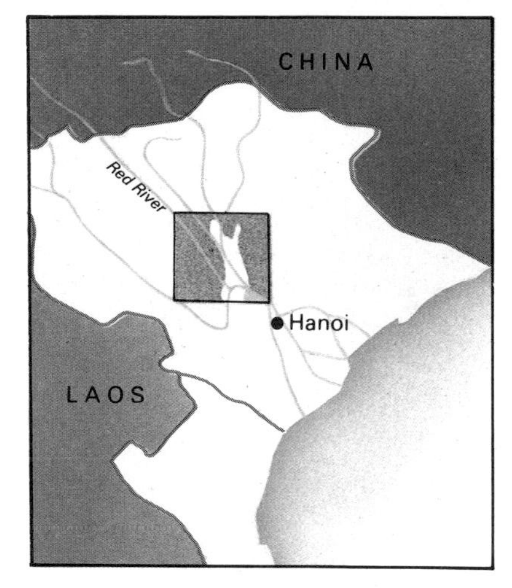

Opposite above: In 1951 Giap made a major miscalculation, and moved over to his third stage of warfare (conventional) too soon. The attacks on the Red River Delta showed that the French still had an advantage in open battle. Opposite below: One of the most important reasons for French success was their ability to switch troops quickly from one point of attack to another, and paratroops were the most mobile troops of all.
Above right: General de Lattre de Tassigny whose tactics paid off handsomely in 1951 and who, perhaps, got more to grips with the central problems posed by revolutionary warfare than any other French commander.
Right and below: If the Red River Delta in 1951 had shown that Giap was capable of making mistakes, so Operation Lorraine *in 1952 showed that the French commanders still found offensive action outside safe areas an almost impossible proposition.*

themselves at the end of long and difficult supply routes and frequently bereft of air and artillery support. The most important area chosen by the Viet Minh for their operations was in the T'ai Highlands to the north-west of Hanoi.

By consolidating their power in this remote area, the Viet Minh were able to build up stocks of weapons and to train their formations for the next big encounter with the French. Meanwhile, guerrilla activity continued across all Vietnam. No French garrison or patrol could relax its vigilance for a moment; no fort or government building, from Hanoi to the Delta, was immune from attack. The grinding strain of maintaining a presence in areas where any peasant might be hostile inevitably affected the morale of the French Army. And in spite of the granting of limited independence to Laos and Cambodia, communist activity increased there too. The French commanders were still unable to formulate a strategy which would enable them to take and maintain the inititiative; yet unless they could find such a strategy, they would inevitably lose the war.

Hoa Binh and Lorraine

In November 1951 de Lattre built up a major mobile force by withdrawing units

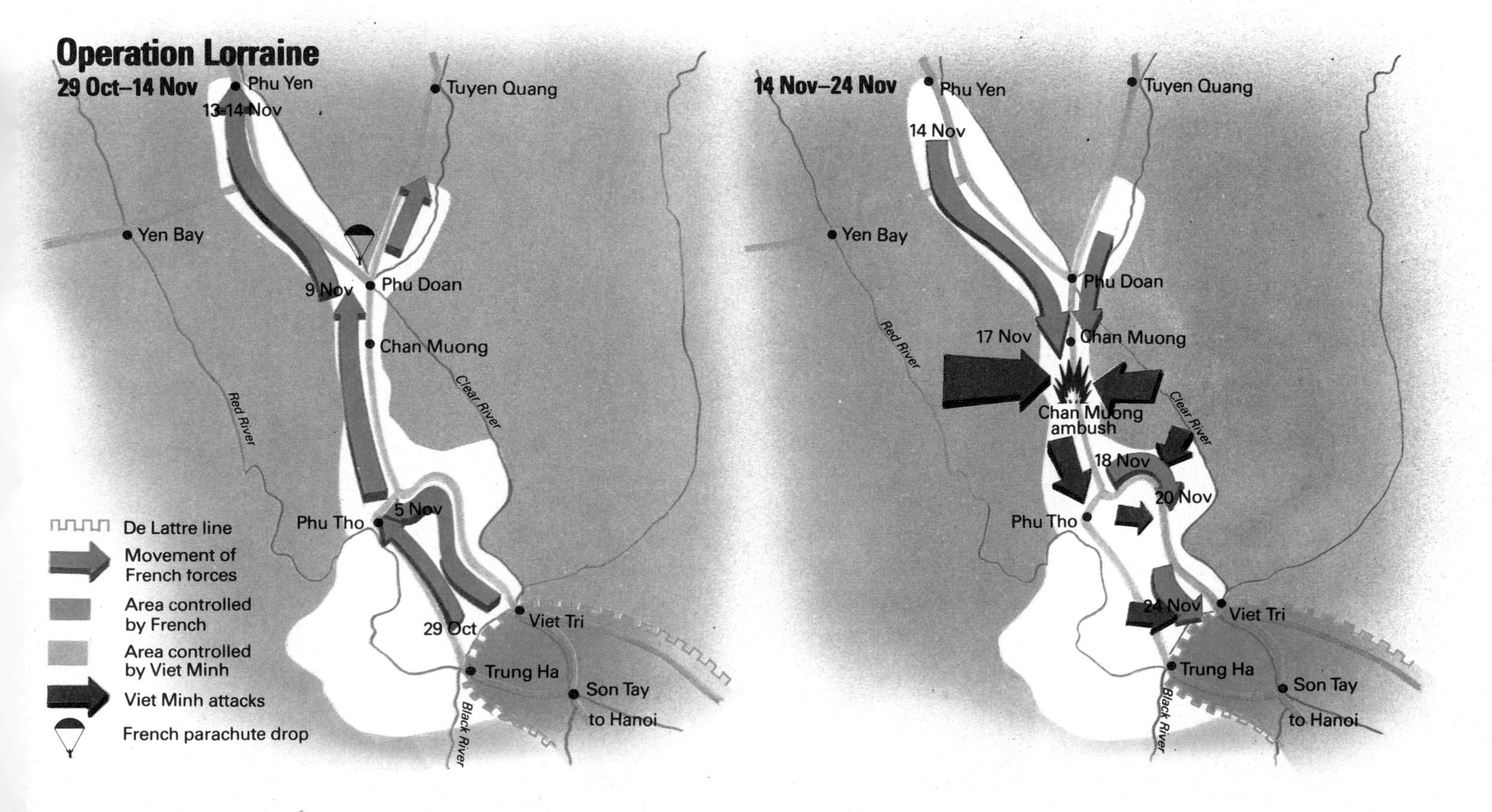

from less critical areas and deployed it in the general area of Hoa Binh on the Black River to the west of Hanoi. The main aim of the task force was to cut the Viet Minh lines of communication, and Hoa Binh lay on a route they had to use to supply their forces as they tried to extend their influence further afield. The Vietnam People's Army (VPA), as the Viet Minh forces were now called, did not fall into the trap of engaging the French in their strongly held positions. Their supply lines were redirected so as to avoid major French garrison areas (easy to do in such rugged country) and instead of grouping to attack in force they adopted the wise ploy of directing their efforts in small groups to cutting off the roads the French needed to keep their troops operational. These tactics paid off handsomely and in February 1952 the French forces in Hoa Binh itself were forced to evacuate their positions.

After the 1952 monsoons General Giap determined to advance through the T'ai Highlands and to reach the Laotian border. He used three divisions for this operation and moved them along a number of well-dispersed lines of advance. To counter this the French, in operation *Lorraine*, mustered a force of over 30,000 troops to move in on the VPA lines of communication and to seek out and destroy their essential reserve supply dumps. This force advanced well over 100 miles (160 km) inside Viet Minh territory and succeeded in finding and destroying a number of dumps though not the most important ones. Giap did not try to mount a major attack on this French force but instead deployed small groups of never more than regimental size to harry and delay French progress. In this he was completely successful. The French had deployed in late October 1952 and by 1 December they were back in their base camps. Giap's forward echelons remained on the Laotian frontier.

The monsoons were still some four to five months off and Giap decided to press on into Laos to link up with the Pathet Lao (the Laotian communist forces). The French were only deployed in small numbers in Laos and there seemed a good chance that the VPA could reach Vientiane, the capital, before the rains set in in May. In response to this move the French, having learnt from their experience in Tonkin, withdrew most of their outlying garrisons in the path of the Viet Minh advance and made a great effort to build up a major defensive position in the Plain of Jars. Every

Below: A French infantryman cautiously examines a road after one of his comrades has been shot. Bottom: No such caution is apparent as a regiment of Viet Minh emerge into a clearing while on their way to the front. Although obviously posed, the photograph demonstrates a major reason for Viet Minh success: the mobility and adaptability of their infantry who always bore the brunt of the fighting.

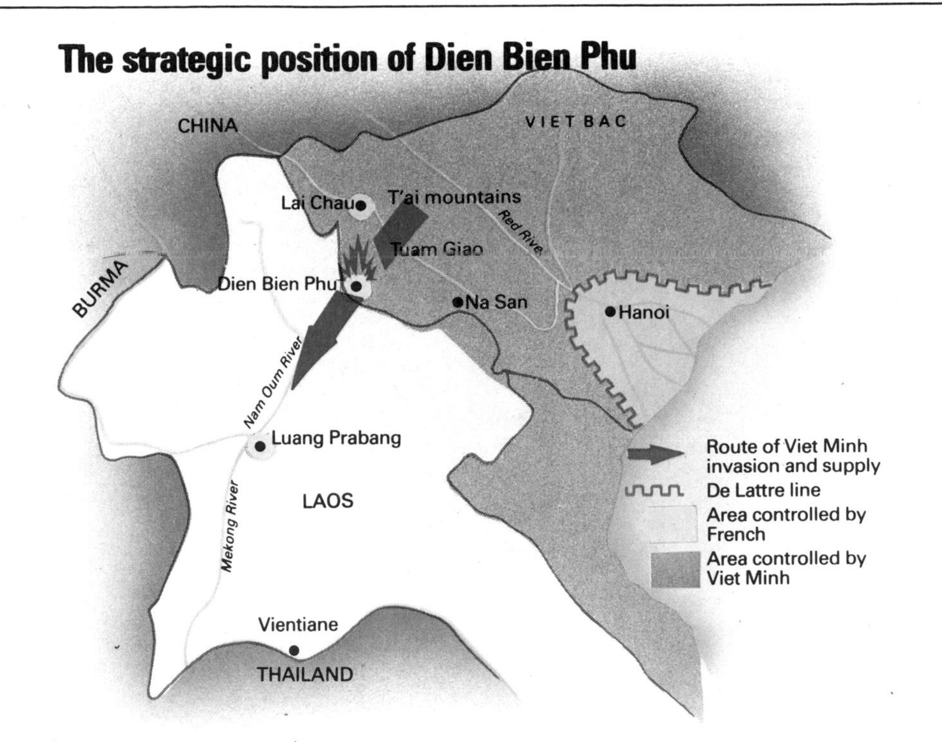

Top: Paratroops, the elite of the French forces, man a 75mm recoilless rifle. These weapons, light and easy to transport, were ideal for mobile warfare. Above: Parachutes open as reinforcements drop in to help the beleaguered garrison at Dien Bien Phu. Above right: To General Navarre, Dien Bien Phu seemed a good battle-ground to meet the Viet Minh because victory there would shatter communist supply lines into Laos.

man and weapon and all tools and defensive stores for this project had to be airlifted from Hanoi and Saigon, distances of 500 and 1000 miles (800 and 1600 km) respectively. In the hope of catching the French before their preparations were complete Giap launched an all-out attack using the best part of two divisions. The French were ready, however, and held the attack without difficulty. The onset of the rains in May 1953 brought an end to the fighting and saw the VPA withdrawing unsuccessfully back to the frontier. This French success on the Plain of Jars should not, however, blind one to the fact that the thinning out of other garrisons to provide this force in Laos had allowed the Viet Minh quietly to extend their influence elsewhere: this steady erosion of the French position was never to be remedied.

Navarre's plans

In July 1953 a new French Commander-in-Chief, General Henri Navarre, arrived in Indochina. His arrival, coinciding with the end of hostilities in Korea and thus the promise of increased aid from the United States, seemed to offer some hope of renewed success for the French forces but in his first report to the French government, soon after arrival, Navarre stated that in his opinion the war could not be won. He made it clear that even to sustain his present position he would need to have further reinforcements. His plea fell on deaf ears and the government in Paris ordered him to defend Laos, if possible, but in so doing not to risk a major defeat of the French Expeditionary Force. It may have been United States pressure to fight against any encroachment of communism, but certainly the French government was not, it seemed, prepared to consider any form of negotiated settlement with the Viet Minh. Such a settlement, even at this late stage, might have salvaged something in the French interest – which was certainly not to be the case later.

To achieve the aims he had been set Navarre withdrew forces from yet more remote garrisons and thereby created a reserve. With this force he executed a succession of rapid small-scale attacks against key points in Viet Minh-held territory. These did little to deter Giap, however, who continued to prepare a major force to advance south into Laos with the optimistic aim of driving as far as Cambodia and thence even south-east into Cochin-China. He launched his offensive in December 1953 and by Christmas Indochina was virtually cut in two at its narrowest point. Giap then turned his attention to northern Laos.

So wide-ranging were the VPA successes and so ineffective were the short sharp French attacks that Navarre decided once again that the French position could only be sustained by building up major garrisons in threatened areas. The biggest of these, positioned to inhibit the advance of the Viet Minh forces into northern Laos, lay on the frontier between Tonkin and Laos; it was located in the area of the small hamlet of Dien Bien Phu.

Navarre originally intended to use Dien Bien Phu to provide assistance in the withdrawal of another garrison to the north and then, after its forces had been built up, as a base from which to carry out long-range patrolling in search of VPA units. However, Dien Bien Phu is strategically placed on main routes from China south into Laos and from Tonkin into Laos and the idea was conceived that the garrison could be reinforced to create such a threat to the Viet Minh that they would be forced to try to neutralize it if they wished to develop their position to the west. This would enable the French to bring them to battle, where superior firepower and tactics would prevail.

The build-up of the base began in November 1953 and by January 1954 some 10,000 men were deployed in the area. There were 12 battalions of infantry, backed by 75mm and 105mm field guns, 155mm howitzers and even 10 light tanks and six fighter-bombers. There were two airfields within the Dien Bien Phu valley and it was intended that they should be used to resupply the garrison from Hanoi, some 170 air miles (270 km) away.

In February 1954 French patrols began to meet enemy forces in close proximity to the Dien Bien Phu perimeter and it quickly became obvious that the VPA was being built up for an attack. Probing actions took place from 11 March and in two night attacks on 13 and 14 March two defended areas to the north fell. The French remained confident, however, not only in their own defensive capability, but of being in a strong position to cause major damage to the bulk of the Viet Minh forces which they now fully expected to be launched into an attack against them.

The French appreciation of their own capability, however, ignored the vulnerability of the aerial lifeline to Hanoi. For the first time in the war the Viet Minh

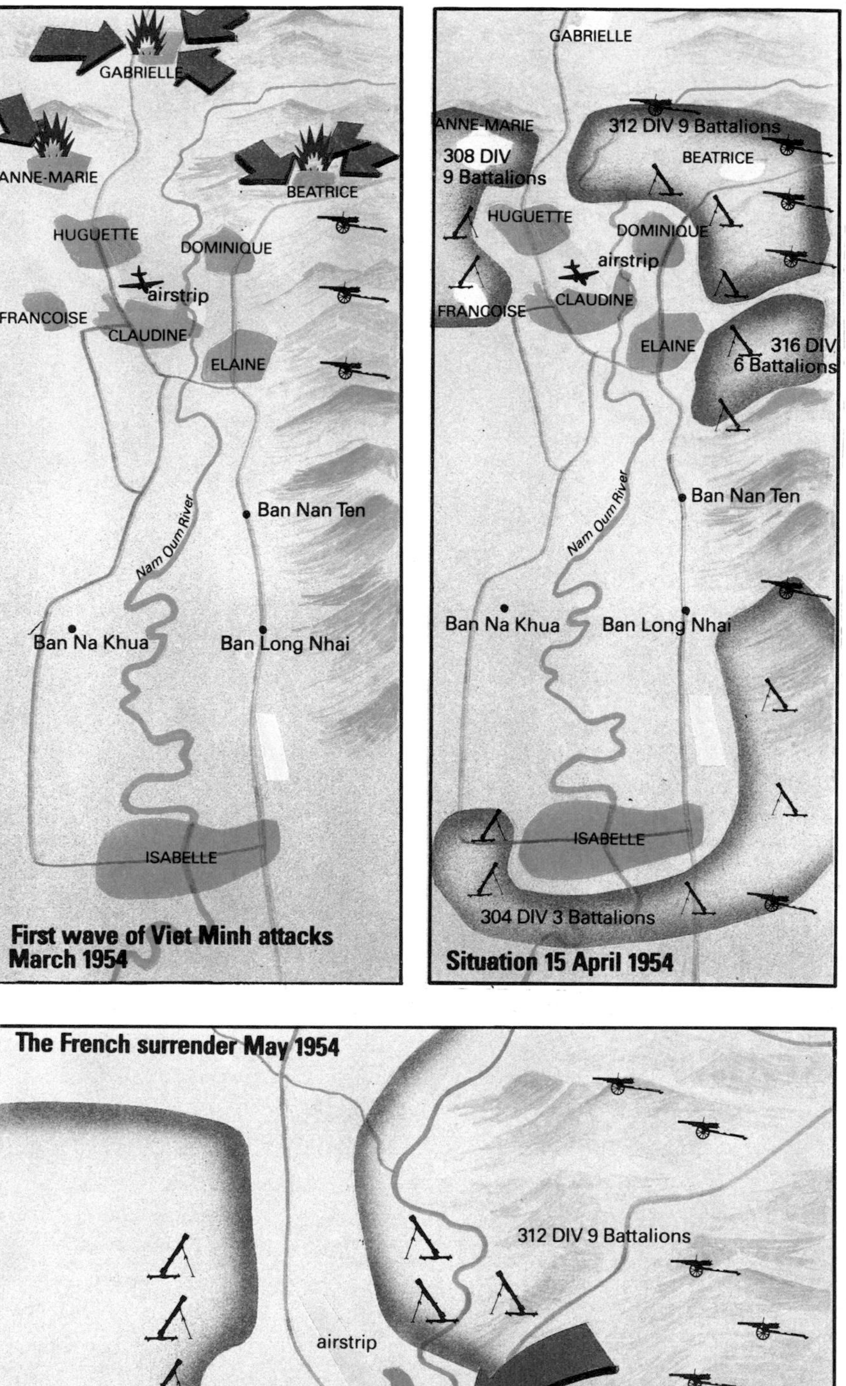

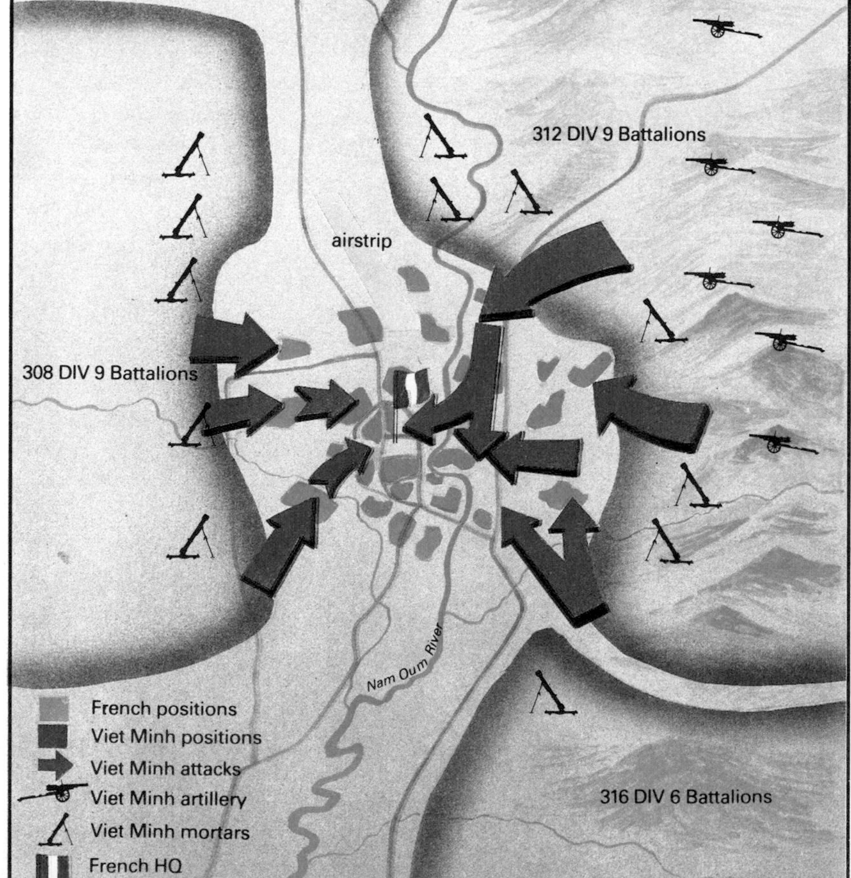

Opposite: The French position at Dien Bien Phu was a series of strongpoints (all given girls' names and supposedly named after the mistresses of one of the French commanders) protecting an airstrip, while to the south of the main position was a further strongpoint ('Isabelle') and an airstrip. The French command had, however, underestimated the weight of artillery which the communists had available; and this artillery that Giap deployed, dug into hillsides and practically immune to air attack, was the key factor. The rapid fall of three strongpoints ('Anne-Marie', 'Gabrielle' and 'Beatrice') practically doomed the whole garrison, but resistance was fierce as the Viet Minh pounded the defences until surrender was inevitable.
Below: Life for the French troops in Dien Bien Phu became a nerve-wracking series of alerts and a physically tiring round of rebuilding defences damaged by artillery fire.
Below right: The Geneva Settlement divided Vietnam at the 17th parallel.

brought into action their 'heavy division' comprising artillery regiments armed with 75mm and 105mm field guns together with a large number of heavy mortars. These weapons were extremely effective against the French troops, who lacked the necessary protection against them. When used against the airfields they soon made them both virtually unusable. When the air-dropping of supplies was introduced the VPA used its second surprise weapon: 16 37mm anti-aircraft guns and a large number of heavy machine-guns. The effect was devastating and when, in March 1954, these weapons were supplemented by further guns the battle was as good as over.

The French surrender

Despite a rapidly deteriorating situation further reinforcements were dropped in to Dien Bien Phu in March and April. They were not able to affect the outcome of the battle, however, and the Viet Minh attacks increased in ferocity. Finally, on 7 May 1954, after a siege lasting 55 days, the French garrison surrendered.

During the siege the Viet Minh advances in others parts of Indochina had continued unabated and it was clear, with the fall of Dien Bien Phu, that the French had lost their last chance of retaining control. In the early months of 1954 moves were afoot to arrange a conference on the future of the area and in April delegates arrived in Geneva for that purpose. The news of the fall of Dien Bien Phu arrived during the course of the conference. The agreement finally reached was that Cambodia and Laos should become independent states pledged to neutrality, and Vietnam should temporarily be divided into two at the 17th parallel of latitude, with the Viet Minh governing the north and with a non-communist government in the south.

The French defeat in Indochina must in part be blamed on policies adopted throughout the war. Successive governments pressed for a military solution yet never provided the troops necessary to achieve it. There seems little doubt that had they gone for a political settlement early on most of their political and economic interests would have remained intact. French commanders-in-chief have been blamed for tying down too many troops in garrisoning provincial centres whose lines of communication were often easily cut. However, every garrison that was abandoned led to a further encroachment by the Viet Minh. It was necessary to hold on to them and, at the same time, to conduct mobile offensive operations, and for this strategy there were never enough troops.

But perhaps the real explanation for the French defeat lay in the unfortunate circumstances which surrounded their return after World War II. They were late on the scene; they met up with an ardent nationalist feeling won over to the communist cause; this movement already had an existing government in the north; and lastly they stood virtually alone and were actively opposed by United States policies immediately after 1945. Only when Red China entered the fray did the American attitude change and, despite generous help thereafter, it was already too late.

2. America Enters the Struggle

US involvement in the tangled affairs of the small Asian country of South Vietnam was a slide down a slippery slope of good intentions and false optimism. South Vietnam had been beset with problems from its very creation as a State. Its ruler, Ngo Van Diem, had been able to overcome many of his opponents and had imposed a strong central rule, but his early successes had not removed the greatest menace the young state faced: communist subversion from within and without. In the early sixties, as Diem's regime tottered under pressure and began to collapse under the weight of its own contradictions, the US government found itself liable for the defence of a weak and vulnerable ally; and as communist success mounted, so the US armed forces were committed to a war very different to any they had experienced before.

Suspected Viet Cong are interrogated by US troops in the An Loc Province

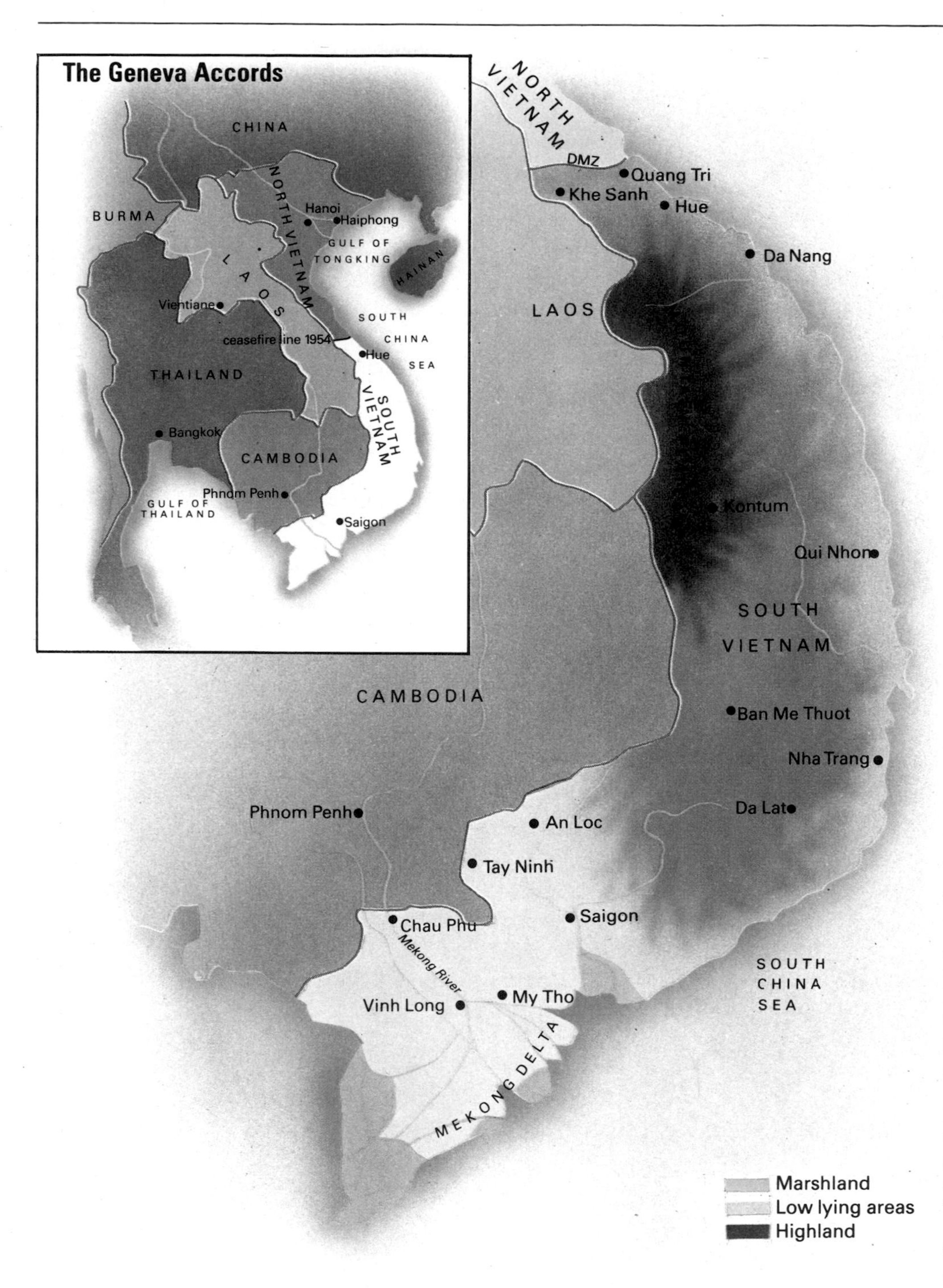

Vietnam was divided into North and South on the 17th parallel by the Geneva Accords of 1954. Many Vietnamese not sympathetic to the communist cause left the North for the South as refugees.

President Eisenhower took office in 1953 at a time of great international tension and domestic trauma. Communist influence seemed to be expanding everywhere abroad, and Senator Joseph McCarthy's witch hunt was rampant at home. Shortly after he took office, Secretary John Foster Dulles articulated the now-famous Domino Theory in a nationwide broadcast: 'If they [the Soviets] could get this peninsula of Indochina, Siam, Burma, Malaya, they would have what is called the rice bowl of Asia. . . . And you can see that if the Soviet Union had control of the rice bowl of Asia that would be another weapon which would tend to expand their control into Japan and into India.'

In the meantime, the war in Indochina had taken an ominous turn; nothing the French could do would redress the balance. The armistice in Korea, signed in late July 1953, relieved China of supplying its forces there, and by the summer the Viet Minh was being amply equipped with sophisticated weapons. Despite Eisenhower's and Dulles's forebodings of the consequences of a communist victory in Indochina, it was becoming clear that the United States would be unable to change the course of events in Vietnam short of American intervention. By the summer of 1953, Washington was torn between the need to keep the French fighting and an inability to convince the French that they would have to promise genuine independence to gain the loyalty of the Vietnamese.

In France, popular unrest was fed by the increasingly desperate military situation in Indochina. As 1953 drew to a close, the bastion at Dien Bien Phu was in serious trouble. The French had committed not only a vast amount of troops and equipment but the prestige of the French Expeditionary Force to the defence of Dien Bien Phu. Eisenhower confronted a stark choice: to provide immediate and massive American aid (including American troops) to the beleaguered French forces, or to stand aside as Paris sought to negotiate its way out at any price.

Under these inauspicious circumstances the foreign ministers of the Soviet Union, the United Kingdom, France, and the United States assembled in Berlin in late January 1954. An international conference to negotiate a permanent settlement of the Korean War was planned for early spring in Geneva, but the French foreign minister pressed for including a discussion of an Indochina settlement. Indeed, it was clear that his government would fall if he returned to Paris without such a commitment. The Americans were fearful of a conference on Indochina, since France's negotiating position was eroding fast. But Eisenhower and Dulles were worried also about possible successor governments in

France. And so the Americans had little choice but to agree that Indochina would be discussed.

The Geneva conference

Throughout February and early March the administration was faced with Congressional reluctance to permit even American maintenance personnel to assist the hard-pressed French forces; sharp differences within the administration and the military establishment on the desirability of American military aid; a restive mood in France; and a disintegrating military situation in Indochina. The forthcoming Geneva conference was of grave concern, and the prospect of Americans negotiating with Chinese communists was especially worrisome to the hard-liners.

The 'Far East conference' convened in Geneva in late April. It 'could not have begun or been conducted under worse conditions', Eisenhower was later to recall. Korea was the first item on the agenda. The discussions were *pro forma;* a ceasefire had already been arranged, and there was little expectation that progress could be made on a final political solution. As the Korean debate drew to a close on 7 May, an usher unobtrusively delivered a note to the French foreign minister. Dien Bien Phu had fallen. The loss of Dien Bien Phu was critical, and although there were still large and powerful French forces fighting elsewhere in Indochina, Paris knew it had lost both the war in Vietnam and its bargaining power in Geneva.

The Indochina phase of the conference was marked by American suspicion and anxiety. The French were desperate for an immediate ceasefire and the British, who together with the Russians chaired the conference, were anxious for one, too. This would have troubled the Americans, in any case. But with Congress still seeking scapegoats for the 'loss of China', the administration was anxious to avoid a major communist diplomatic victory in South-east Asia.

The American delegation sulked its way through the sessions and during the final, critical stage virtually ignored the proceedings altogether. But an agreement of sorts was reached – an agreement which was more than the French could have hoped for in the light of their military defeat, and was considerably less than the Viet Minh had expected in the light of their victory. The final declaration promised to accomplish little more than to give an international blessing to the independence of Laos and Cambodia and to establish two political entities in Vietnam. It was not signed by any of the delegations, and was opposed by the two most directly affected – the non-communist and communist Vietnamese representatives. And the United States, in a unilateral statement, disassociated itself from the declaration, although it promised to abide by it.

A nation divided

It is not certain what the delegates to the Geneva conference had in mind about the future of Vietnam after the French left. An election was scheduled for 1956 after which the two parts of the country were to be reunited under a 'freely elected' national leader. But the election was not held. The regime in Hanoi and its sympathizers elsewhere place the onus on the Saigon regime and the United States. South Vietnamese and American officials blame the communists in Vietnam whose concept of 'free elections' would have guaranteed a defeat for the Saigon

Above: Ngo Dinh Diem was appointed prime minister of South Vietnam in 1954 and in the following year assumed the role of president. Below: In spite of the 1954 ceasefire, intermittent guerrilla warfare continued – here a Vietnamese fishing boat is searched by South Vietnamese security forces for contraband and arms.

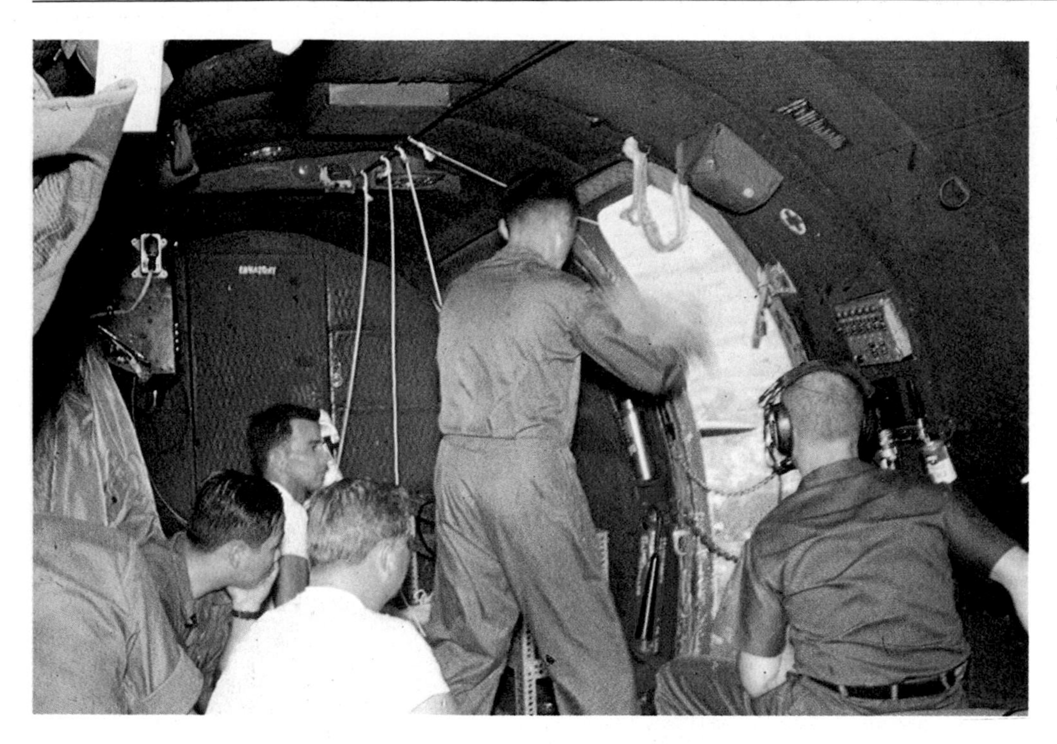

Left: Psychological warfare leaflets are dropped from a C-47 aircraft over an area of South Vietnam thought to be inhabited by Viet Cong insurgents.

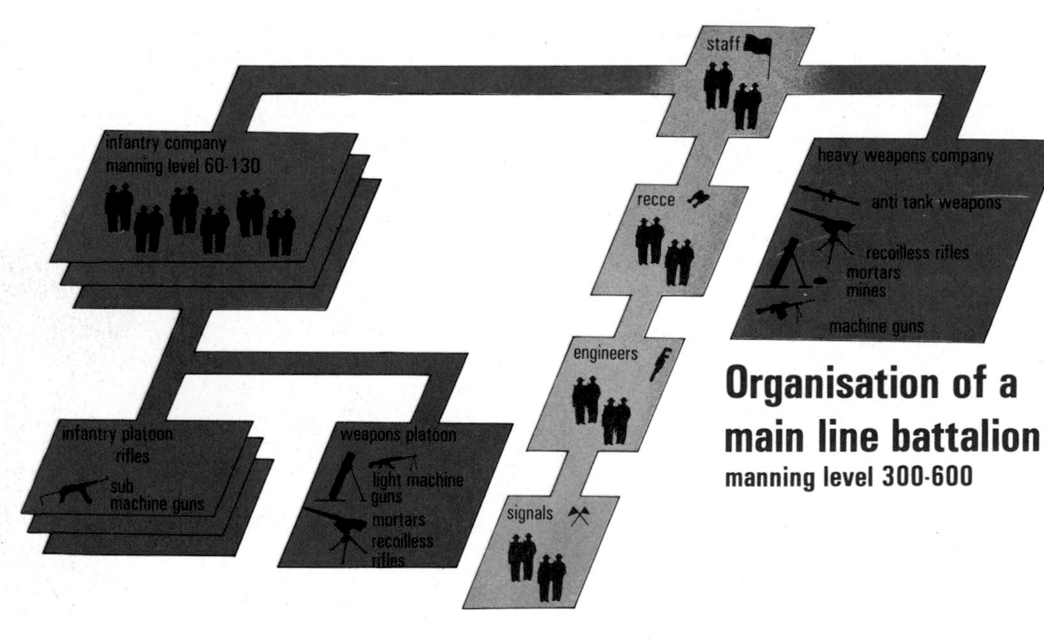

Left: The structure of a Viet Cong battalion. Not until the early sixties were VC units as well armed and organized as this one shown here.
Opposite top: Viet Cong guerrillas off-duty but with weapons – an SKS rifle and AK47 assault rifle – at the ready. Opposite centre: Communist guerrillas prepare a punji-stick booby trap. Opposite below: General Vo Nguyen Giap, leading military theorist of North Vietnam's struggle to overthrow the government of the South.

government. In any case, the two parts of Vietnam were to be divided at the 17th parallel – like Germany and Korea, one country, but two nations. The North was ruled by a communist government headed by Ho Chi Minh; the South, by a non-communist government headed by Ngo Dinh Diem.

The saga of Diem is a dramatic one. In 1953 he was a virtual recluse in Catholic monasteries in the United States; in 1954 he became South Vietnam's prime minister; a year later he was president of South Vietnam; and in 1963 he was murdered in a coup. There is still considerable controversy about the American role in the rise and fall of Diem. Some claim he was handpicked to lead a non-communist Vietnam by John Foster Dulles and was eventually betrayed by John F. Kennedy. Others maintain Diem was the choice of the non-communist Vietnamese themselves; he had impeccable anti-French credentials; he was an ardent Catholic, and generally regarded as incorruptible. The truth will never be known; everyone who could shed light on it has long since died. But however it was that Diem found himself heading the government of South Vietnam, he was soon given American endorsement and, as the years went by, an increasing amount of American economic and military aid. Indeed, Washington became so politically committed to Diem by the late 1950s that Eisenhower and later Kennedy probably needed Diem as much as he needed American support.

Diem takes over

Diem's return to Vietnam turned out to be a nightmare. The French and Emperor Bao Dai – chosen as president – were soon plotting his removal; religious sects were warring against each other and against the government; and powerful hoodlums who controlled both the police and crime in Saigon took arms against him. By then southern communist rebels, known as the Viet Cong (VC), were ravaging the countryside. In May 1955 Washington concluded that it would have to give Diem unequivocal political backing and tangible assistance or its hopes to create a strong non-communist counter to Ho Chi Minh in the North would be lost. 'The United States has great sympathy for a nationalist cause that is free and effective,' the administration announced. 'For this reason we have been and are continuing to support the legal government of Ngo Dinh Diem.' This turned out to be a watershed. There was now no turning back.

By the end of 1955 Diem had achieved most of the objectives he had originally set. The power of the religious sects was broken; the hoodlums were defeated; French influence was virtually eliminated; Bao Dai was deposed. The one goal he was not to achieve during 1955 was one he would never achieve – the creation of a strong and popular anti-communist government.

Diem's policies and programmes from 1956 onward were leading to disaster, but the trend was not apparent to most observers. The chaos in other ex-colonial areas of Asia and Africa and the corrupt governments in Latin America made South Vietnam and its leader look very good in comparison. In mid-1956, Senator John F. Kennedy noted that South Vietnam had virtually disappeared from the American newspapers and that 'the American people have all but forgotten' Vietnam. This was, in part, due to 'the amazing success of President Diem in meeting . . . the major political and economic crises which heretofore continually plagued Vietnam.' Kennedy then read his own fortune: 'in my opinion, Vietnam would in all likelihood be receiving more attention from our Congress and administration, and greater assistance under our aid programs, if it were in imminent danger of communist invasion or revolution'.

Much of the reporting from Saigon was coloured by the fervour of a small band of Americans who looked upon Diem as a latter-day Saint Joan. There were, however, hints of discontent with Diem's methods of rule, impatience with his tendency to lecture rather than inspire, and unease in the face of communist forays. It was soon evident that despite economic and social advances, Diem lacked two important, ultimately critical, qualities: he was unable to gain the support of the urban population, and he was incapable of stemming the erosion of security in the countryside and even in Saigon. In late October 1957 there was a portent of the dark days to come. Terrorists bombed the United States Information Service Library and an American barracks; 13 American soldiers were injured.

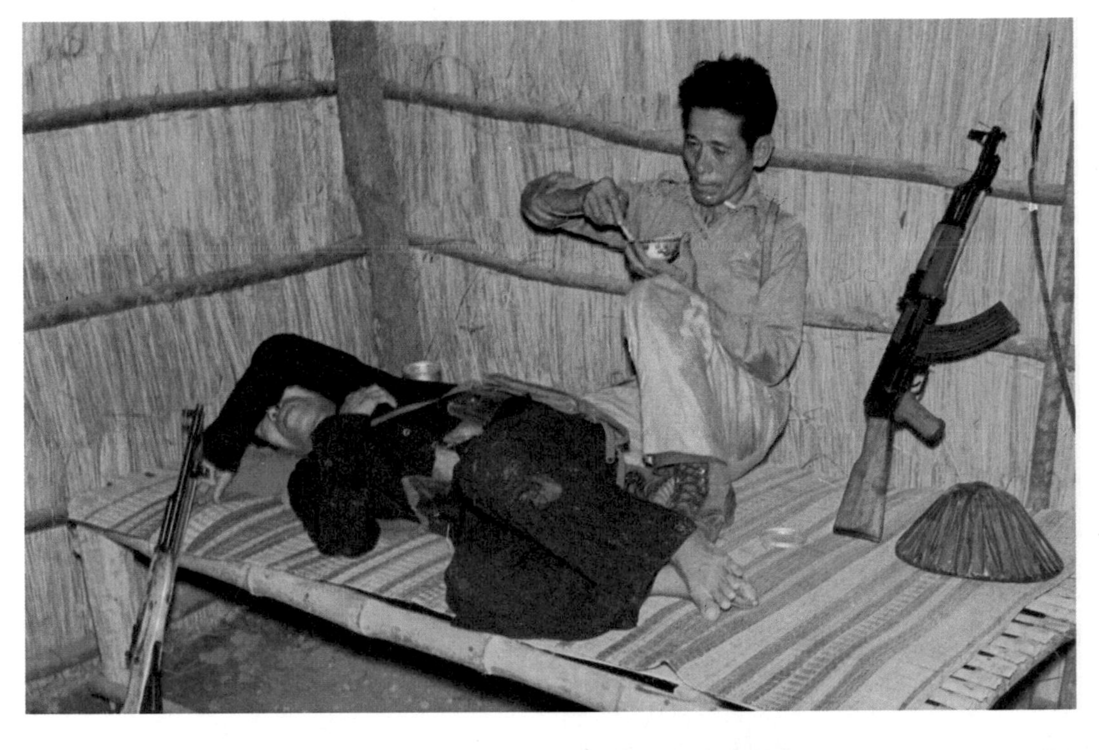

A family in power

Meanwhile, Diem was suppressing Vietnamese newspapers which criticized him, and members of the Ngo family were becoming conspicuously powerful and objectionable. Indeed, Diem had become little more than a façade, with the real power exercised by his three brothers, none of whom held any official position: Nhu, the 'adviser' in the presidential palace; Can, the virtual warlord of central Vietnam; and Archbishop Thuc, who wielded substantial influence

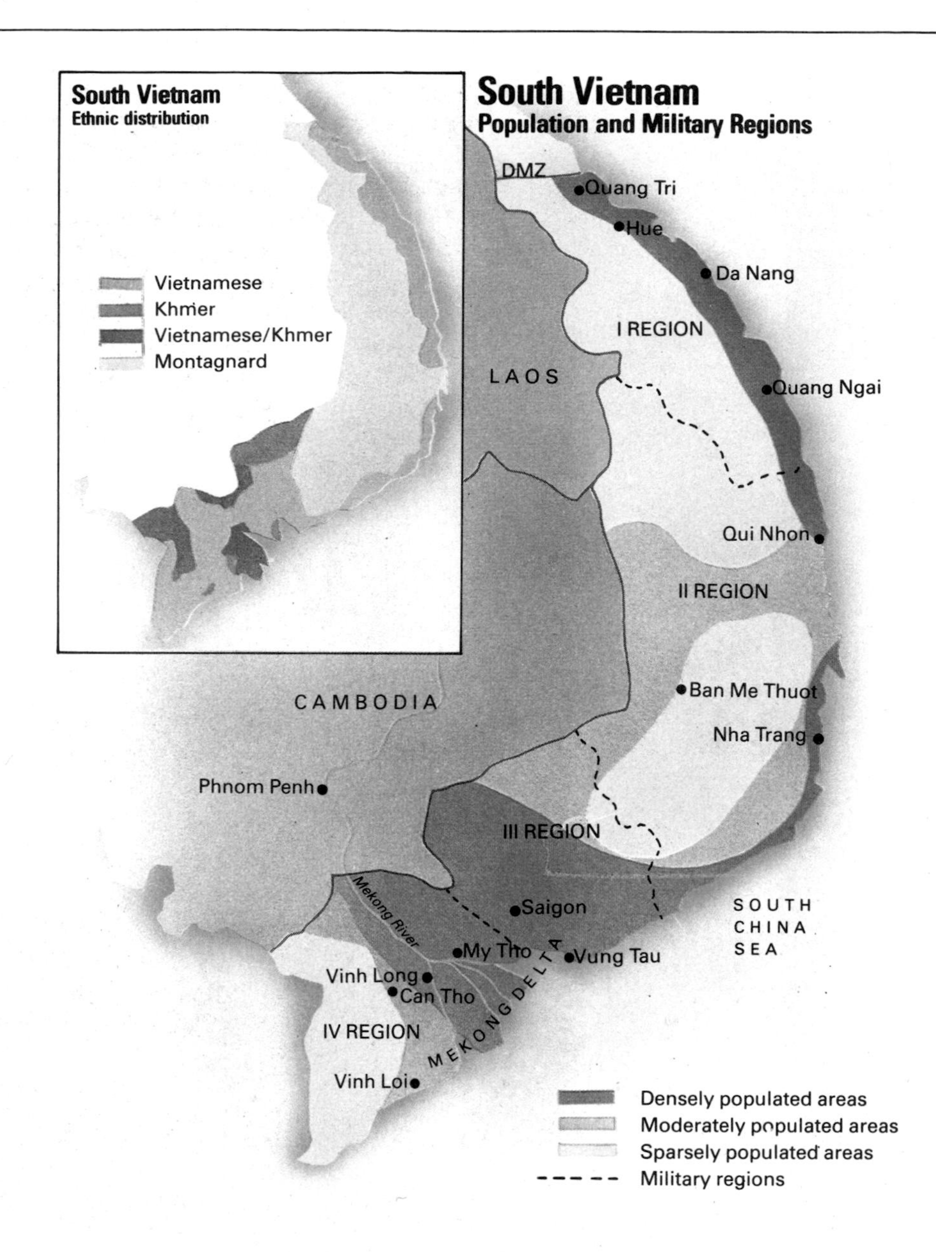

through his control over the vocal and powerful Catholic minority. And behind the men behind the scenes was the beauteous and clever Madame Nhu.

By 1959, South Vietnam was threatened not so much by an invasion of what was now called the North Vietnamese Army (NVA) as by hit-and-run guerrilla and propaganda actions throughout the land. South Vietnamese divisions, in static defence positions along the 17th parallel, sopped up much of Diem's available military manpower and equipment and diverted much-needed protection from communist terrorism in the rural areas.

The threat was given an added dimension by the infusion of well-trained specialists in military and political warfare from North Vietnam. The young men who had gone north after the Geneva settlement of 1954 were beginning to come 'home'. They were now skilled in the techniques of radio communication, ordnance repair, sabotage, and propaganda. By early 1959, the security situation had deteriorated to the point that Diem established drumhead courts to mete out death sentences not only to terrorists and members of subversive organizations, but to speculators and 'rumour spreaders'. Events moved rapidly and for the worse in 1960 when thousands of Viet Cong were creating havoc throughout large areas of the countryside.

As the grumbling of the population about both communist terror and Diem's counter-terror increased. Diem reverted to the meditative, cloistered life that had been part of his recent past. His strong sense of idealism and confidence in his own political instincts made him even less inclined to listen, let alone accede, to American advice and blandishments. It was this stubbornness that planted the seeds of his own destruction.

The Kennedy policy

President Kennedy's inheritance on 21 January 1961 was an American commitment in Vietnam. While less specific in form and smaller in substance than it later became, it was nonetheless so concrete and substantial that American prestige was tied to the declining fortunes of Ngo Dinh Diem. By mid-1961, there were 12,000 hard-core communist guerrillas and almost 60 per cent of South Vietnam was believed to be under some degree of communist control. Kennedy was uneasy about whether South Vietnam could make any real progress against the strength of the Viet Cong guerrillas as long as Diem and Nhu regarded the struggle as a personal, holy war. Vice-President Johnson was sent on a fact-finding trip.

The adrenalin Johnson injected into the Saigon regime had only a temporary effect; lassitude and uncertainty soon again became dominant. In September, the Viet Cong seized a provincial capital about 50 miles (80 km) from Saigon, decapitated the province chief, and scurried into the jungle before government troops arrived. President Kennedy told the United Nations that Vietnam was 'under attack', and a few days later Diem proclaimed that there was a 'real war' raging in South Vietnam. Throughout the summer there had been much talk in Washington of sending American combat troops to South-east Asia, and by October several plans had been worked out for direct American intervention.

It was against this background that President Kennedy sent his military adviser, Maxwell Taylor, to Saigon to appraise the security of Vietnam. On his return, General Taylor told the president that communist subversion and guerrilla war were succeeding. Taylor recommended a 'massive joint effort' in which the American representatives would participate 'actively' in government administration, military plans and operations, intelligence, and flood relief.

In the end, the administration decided against sending combat troops to Vietnam. The decision reflected concern for the delicate negotiations on Laos then taking place in Geneva, and a feeling that, in the last analysis, fighting the Viet Cong was a South Vietnamese job. It was decided, however, to increase American military assistance. A large number of American advisers and a substantial amount of military equipment, including helicopters with their crews, were sent to Vietnam.

The US build-up

The early months of 1962 saw a quickening of American support. In his State of the Union message to Congress, the president expressed his hopes and concerns: 'A satisfactory settlement in Laos would also help to achieve and safeguard the peace in Vietnam, where the foe is increasing his tactics of terror, where our own efforts have been stepped up, and where the local government has initiated new programs and reforms – the systematic aggression now bleeding that country is not a "war of national liberation" for Vietnam is already free. It is a war of attempted subjugation – and it will be resisted.'

Above: President John F. Kennedy is sworn into office. In his inaugural address he claimed that America would 'pay any price, bear any burden, meet any hardship, support any friend, oppose any foe to assure the survival and success of liberty.' Right: Dean Rusk, Secretary of State in the Kennedy administration. Below Right: Secretary of Defense Robert McNamara who spearheaded the drive to increase America's military potential.
Opposite top: Population distribution in South Vietnam. Ethnic antagonism was a contributory factor in the inability of the South Vietnam government to put up a united front against communism. Opposite below: Ho Chi Minh – his ruthless planning provided a firm foundation for communist strategy during the war.

To demonstrate the seriousness of the administration, a new American military headquarters – the Military Assistance Command, Vietnam (MACV) – was established in Saigon in early February. Washington was now acknowledging that between 2000 and 4000 American troops were already in Vietnam, although the administration stressed that they were 'not in combat'. The issue of whether Americans were merely advising Vietnamese forces or participating in combat operations opened a fissure between the American press and the administration. This was widened further by conflicting interpretations and assessments of political and military developments. As the American involvement grew, so did the size and interest of the press corps in Saigon. Doubting voices were raised.

Meanwhile, the war was not going well. The Army of the Republic of South Vietnam (ARVN) was not taking kindly to American advice, and Diem was not following through on promises to liberalize his regime. The Buddhists, long-suffering under the French, were beginning to assert themselves against the stubborn and conspiratorial rule of Diem and his family. In spite of inexperience in practical politics, the Buddhist hierarchy had an instinct for public relations, an uncanny sense of timing, and great courage. This, plus years of being treated as second-class citizens in a country where they vastly outnumbered the Catholics, drove them to the ramparts.

By mid-June 1963, the Buddhist crisis was tearing apart Hué and Saigon and was having major reverberations throughout the rest of Vietnam. Government troops were diverted from military operations against the communists to cope with street demonstrations, guard government buildings, and isolate the pagodas. The universities and high schools of Hué and Saigon became centres of dissension and the world was made uncomfortably aware of the problem when Buddhist priests began to burn themselves to death in the streets. The Saigon government devoted itself to the Buddhist challenge.

Diem's own incompetence, the increasing influence of Nhu and Madame Nhu, the deteriorating security situation, and the Buddhist unrest were now preoccupying officials in Washington. There were 12,000 American military advisers in Vietnam, and the administration had a high stake in stability and progress against the Viet Cong. By August, after a brutal raid by Diem's elite troops against a principal Buddhist pagoda, Washington's patience had run thin. The State Department issued a stern warning: 'The action represents a direct violation by the Vietnamese Government of assurances that it was pursuing a policy of reconciliation with the Buddhists. The United States deplores repressive actions of this nature.' Washington accompanied this by a veiled threat to withdraw American troops.

In the meantime, the Vietnamese generals were plotting the overthrow of the Diem regime. Their feelers for American support brought polite interest, but no commitment. By late summer, there was virtually no communication between Ambassador Henry Cabot Lodge and the presidential palace, and American policy was at a critical point of decision. Secretary of Defense Robert McNamara and General Taylor were sent to make a report. It was melancholy and pessimistic, although the White House softened the impact of their findings with an optimistic prediction of early military victories.

Diem falls

As part of a final effort to apply pressure on Diem in the late summer and early autumn, the administration cancelled its funding of Nhu's special forces and curtailed other aid programmes as well. Although such pressures had little tangible effect on the course of events in Vietnam during the last critical weeks of October, they did have a major psychological effect. For the first time since 1954, the United States had taken a conspicuous, definitive step to demonstrate its opposition to the policies of the Saigon regime. Most importantly, it provided a clear signal to those Vietnamese opposing Diem that the United States was not automatically, irrevocably, committed to President Diem. The denouement took place soon after.

A group of generals and colonels representing key elements of the Vietnamese armed forces attacked the palace during the siesta hour of 1 November. Diem and Nhu refused to surrender. Many hours later, after ascertaining that the support they thought they could rely on had melted away, the brothers escaped to a house in the Chinese section of the city. They gave themselves up in the early morning of the following day, and were shot while being taken to the generals' headquarters.

The United States did not overtly support the coup, but it must have been clear to the generals by September that Washington was not opposed to a change. Planning for the coup had taken place since the summer and, although rumours were rife, the Americans were kept in the dark until early October when the gener-

Opposite top: US Army instructors demonstrate hand-to-hand combat to South Vietnamese Rangers. Opposite below: Well camouflaged North Vietnamese lorries carry supplies to communists fighting in South Vietnam.
Above right: Viet Cong traps were ingenious and deadly – this one is a spiked trap suspended above a door to swing down at chest height. Centre right: An entrance to a Viet Cong bunker discovered by American troops in South Vietnam. Below: A complex tunnel system showing the various traps employed by the Viet Cong.

als involved told a trusted American about their plans. He kept the American ambassador closely informed and the ambassador, in turn, reported the developments to the White House. But few other officials were aware of what was about to transpire.

Among the generals involved were several who were to have their moment in the political sun during the months to follow. But their power would be shortlived. Within a few years, most were destined to go into exile and oblivion. They were unable to remain on the slippery seat of power in the face of ambitious rival claimants or because they exceeded even the high tolerance of the Vietnamese people for corruption and ineffectiveness. But two members of this group were to have a longer staying power than their colleagues.

Ky and Thieu

Air Marshal Nguyen Cao Ky and General Nguyen Van Thieu were both junior officers in the French Army of Indochina.

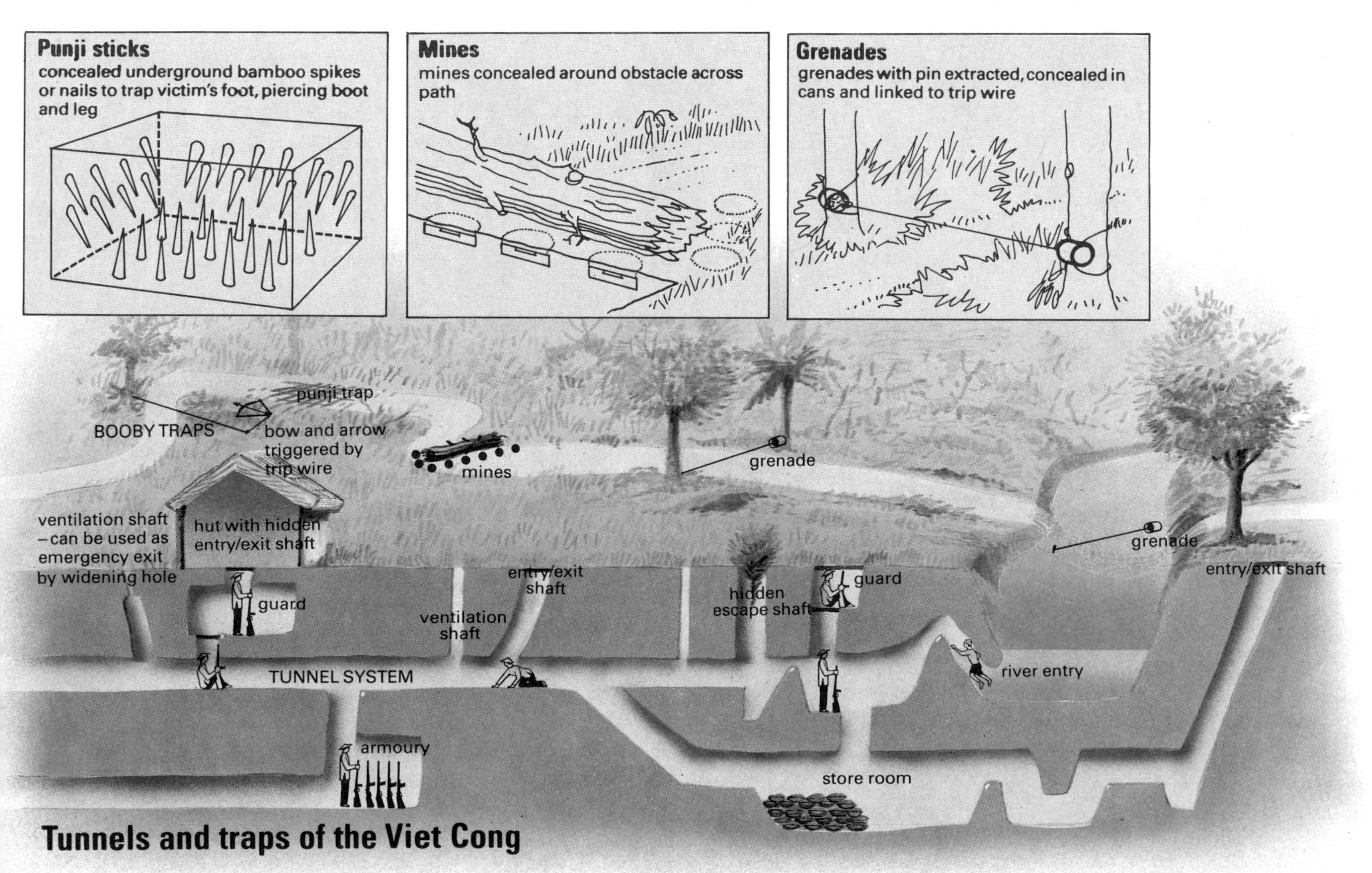

Tunnels and traps of the Viet Cong

Both rose quickly to senior posts in the Vietnam military establishment after independence. Both were young, ambitious, and bright. But there the resemblance ended. Ky was flamboyant and outgoing; Thieu was withdrawn, socially conservative, something of a 'loner'. After the other generals were to have their brief fling at power and glory it would be these two men who would take over. By 1964, Ky and Thieu divided the responsibility of running Vietnam between them, but after a few years of jockeying for position the quiet Thieu came out on top and the flashy Ky faded from the limelight. Thieu was to retain his power for more than a decade. But all of this was yet to come. On that November day in 1963, none of the participants in the coup had any specific idea what would transpire after Diem and his family were removed. Indeed, it was this uncertainty, this lack of planning, which was to lead to early trouble.

President Kennedy was assassinated soon after Diem was murdered. And so the end of 1963 was marked by new governments in both Saigon and Washington. President Johnson had a host of problems to preoccupy him during that dark period of late 1963 and early 1964. Vietnam, he felt, would have to ride along under the existing policy of large-scale American aid but no intervention. In Saigon meanwhile, the political situation, momentarily brightened by the sudden change of government, soon deteriorated as a series of incompetent military juntas succeeded each other. During 1964 alone, six governments held office. Washington was becoming increasingly frustrated, but put the best face it could on each new regime, and American economic assistance and military aid increased as the months went by.

McNamara and the Maddox

With the South Vietnamese high command concentrating on politics rather than on fighting off the ever-increasing strength of the insurgents, the military situation went from bad to worse. Secretary McNamara and other high administration officials were virtually commuting back and forth from Washington to Saigon to keep tabs on the deteriorating condition of America's stake in political stability and a military victory.

The first half of 1964 was marked by growing doubts stemming from the daily erosion of the situation in Vietnam. Planning was proceeding in Washington against various military contingencies. In line with the findings that followed McNamara's various trips to Vietnam, more American advisers were dispatched, more equipment was sent, large numbers of helicopters and pilots were deployed, and an intensive effort was mounted to patrol the approaches to Vietnam along the Laos border, the 17th parallel, and the coast of Vietnam. It was this latter enterprise that was to present Johnson with the sharpest crisis thus far in his tenure of office – one that was to haunt his administration until the day in 1969 when he boarded the plane for Texas and retirement.

On 2 August 1964, the American destroyer *Maddox* was steaming in the Gulf of Tonkin, 30 miles (50 km) off the coast of Vietnam. Although the *Maddox* was clearly in international waters, the Gulf is bordered by North Vietnam, the China mainland, and Hainan Island. Hanoi and Peking looked upon the Gulf of Tonkin as being a sensitive, virtually private preserve.

The *Maddox* was on a surveillance and intelligence-collection mission when it was fired upon by three North Vietnamese torpedo boats. The destroyer and a few American planes struck back, damaging the attacking craft. President Johnson was enraged, but the official reaction from Washington was mild and low-key. 'I have instructed the Navy', the president said on 3 August, '1) to continue the patrols . . . 2) to double the force by adding an additional destroyer . . . 3) to provide a combat air patrol . . . 4) to attack with the objective . . . of destroying [attacking forces].'

On the following day, yet another American destroyer in the Gulf reported being under attack. The circumstances were obscure and there was some initial doubt that the radar and other warning devices were being reliably read. In the event, the president ordered 'air action . . .

Opposite far left: President Nguyen Van Thieu assumed power in South Vietnam in 1964 after a series of short-lived and ineffectual governments that followed the assassination of President Diem. Opposite left: The summary execution of a Viet Cong officer by a Saigon police chief. Pictures such as these offended American liberal sensibilities and became useful propaganda for the anti-war movement. Above: General William C. Westmoreland, shortly before taking over as US military commander in Vietnam on 20 June 1964. Above right: The American destroyer Maddox *which was attacked by North Vietnamese torpedo boats in the Gulf of Tonkin.*

against gunboats and certain supporting facilities' in North Vietnam. Sixty-four sorties were flown against the torpedo bases and an oil storage area nearby.

Power for the president

The Tonkin Gulf incident was a watershed for President Johnson. In a joint resolution, Congress gave the president virtually unanimous support for wide-ranging powers – support especially important in an election year. But the circumstances surrounding the whole affair sowed seeds of mistrust that would poison the relations between the president and many members of Congress, as well as between the administration and the American public. There was a lingering uneasiness that the evidence on which a decision to attack North Vietnam had been based was less than conclusive.

Few senators or congressmen realized in the excitement of the Tonkin Gulf attacks that they would be surrendering so much of their influence on the future course of events in Vietnam by passing the joint resolution in the form suggested by the administration. The resolution was so comprehensive that, 18 months later, when the question of a declaration of war by Congress was raised, the legal adviser of the State Department concluded that 'further Congressional action was not required'.

Having retaliated against North Vietnam, the administration reverted to the pre-Tonkin strategy of limiting the fighting to the South. President Johnson, now on the campaign trail, had to put the best face he could on his Vietnam policy. He was being accused of having a 'no-win' policy. It was hard to demonstrate that an early victory in Vietnam was likely, but in late October good news came from Saigon. A provisional constitution had been completed and a civilian government installed. But Washington's satisfaction was shortlived. At the end of October, virtually on the eve of the American elections, the Viet Cong struck its hardest blow to date – against American forces at Bien Hoa, the largest United States air base in Vietnam. Six American B-57 jet bombers were destroyed, and 23 American soldiers were killed or wounded. Ambassador Maxwell Taylor recommended retaliation against North Vietnam, but Washington refused.

By early 1965, American policy was clearly floundering. Some officials in Washington were even advocating an overall strategy that would permit the United States 'to lose more slowly', in the hope that a South Vietnamese government could be organized that would eventually be able to compete politically with the National Liberation Front (NLA), the political arm of the Viet Cong.

In late January, the president sent his special assistant, McGeorge Bundy, and other civilian and military officials to Vietnam. They were to return with recommendations on whether the United

States should phase out, continue its policy of assisting the South Vietnamese, or intervene directly. The Viet Cong insurgents made the decision for them. On 7 February they attacked an American military barracks, killed eight Americans, and wounded more than 100. The president's statement issued soon after the attack was the beginning of a long, difficult, bloody journey: 'On 7 February, US and South Vietnamese air elements were directed to launch retaliatory attacks against barracks and staging areas in the southern area of North Viet-Nam – used by Hanoi for training and infiltration of Viet Cong personnel into South Viet Nam. . . .'

Reactions to the bombing

The inception of the American bombing campaign created a tremendous outcry, both abroad and at home. As part of an effort to enlist foreign and domestic understanding and support, the White House was obsessed with the need to widen international military and economic aid for the government of South Vietnam. Korea, Australia, New Zealand, Thailand and the Philippines ultimately sent 65,000 troops to Vietnam. Although this was a significant force, it was of greater political than military importance to Washington. The allied military commitment relieved some of the American sense of international isolation. Although the American effort was rationalized by 'SEATO (South East Asia Treaty Organisation) obligations', this rationale was more cosmetic than real. Of the seven member countries, three – Pakistan, France and the United Kingdom – were not represented in Vietnam, and Korea, the largest troop contributor aside from the United States, was not a member of SEATO.

The American bombing of North Vietnam may have improved the morale of the South Vietnamese in the urban areas, but it probably made little difference in the countryside – and it had little effect on the political situation in Saigon, where the generals continued to squabble. Meanwhile, the military situation continued to deteriorate. The ARVN avoided engagements wherever possible. When they confronted the enemy, the Viet Cong won the day, more often than not.

April turned out to be a fateful month. The White House approved a wide range of new steps, from psychological warfare to increased American troop deployments, but recommendations for extending the bombing to Hanoi were rejected. The president agreed to send approximately 20,000 troops and two additional Marine battalions to Vietnam, and to permit the Marine units guarding major installations to engage in active combat.

The early spring of 1965 was not only a time of decision with respect to an American ground force commitment to Vietnam; it also marked country-wide stirrings within the United States on the peace front. The president started his own efforts to seek a peaceful settlement on 25 March: 'The United States will never be second in seeking a settlement in Viet-Nam that is based on an end of communist aggression. . . . I am ready to go anywhere at any time, and meet with anyone whenever there is promise of progress toward an honorable peace.' This was followed by another speech in April in which the president reiterated his desire for peace with a proposal for a vast economic development programme for South-east Asia, including North Vietnam, once the fighting stopped. On the next day, Hanoi released its own peace package: the United States must withdraw from South Vietnam and cease its 'acts of war' against North Vietnam; pending unification, North and South Vietnam must agree that no foreign bases or troops be allowed on their soil and that they will join no military alliances; the internal affairs of South Vietnam must be settled in accordance with the programmes of the National Liberation Front; the reunification of Vietnam must be settled by the Vietnamese themselves without outside interference. And thus began a dialogue of the deaf which was to continue for many years.

Ground troops go in

Communist strength had increased substantially during the first few months of 1965. By the end of April, approximately 100,000 Viet Cong irregulars and more

Top: Troops of the Royal Australian Regiment leap from US helicopters on their return from a battalion-strength operations in South Vietnam. Centre: Presidential assistant McGeorge Bundy on a fact-finding mission, discusses the political situation with South Vietnam's Chief of State Phan Khac Suu in February 1965. Above: The other side of the coin – Viet Cong guerrillas march past a destroyed tank after a successful raid.

than 40,000 main force troops, including a full battalion of regular NVA troops, were operating in South Vietnam. And by early May, 45,000 American troops had been deployed.

Pressure for more American combat troops continued to grow. Despite the air strikes against enemy concentrations in the South and against targets in the North, the communists continued to hold the military initiative. At a news conference on 9 July, President Johnson prepared the country for possible new major military steps: 'The incidents are going up. The casualties are going up . . . it will get worse before it gets better. . . . Our manpower needs there are increasing, and will continue to do so. . . . Whatever is required I am sure will be supplied.'

The president told a nationwide television audience in late July that American fighting forces in Vietnam would be increased from 75,000 to 125,000 men, and further increases would be ordered as required. Several days after this announcement he indicated he would ask Congress for additional defence appropriations. The 700 million dollars authorized three months before was already committed; an additional 1.7 billion dollars was requested for the remaining budget year. Congress approved the request.

The ensuing months of 1965 were cheerless. Even in the face of the increasing build-up of American forces in South Vietnam and the intensified bombing of the North, the enemy still seemed unimpressed and unaffected. By the autumn, the war began to intrude seriously on the normal life of Americans. Draft calls had increased substantially and American casualties were being felt across the country. Opposition to the war became more shrill and more organized.

The ceasefire at Christmas 1965 was extended through January in the hope of inducing Hanoi to come to the negotiating table. American officials were sent on a highly publicized international 'flying circus' to demonstrate American good faith. But there was no response from Hanoi. By the end of January 1966 the bombing of North Vietnam was resumed with renewed intensity, and additional forces were deployed. By June 265,000 American troops were already in Vietnam and 18,000 were on the way. In addition, 50,000 American naval personnel were in the area. Congress approved yet another supplementary appropriation for Vietnam – this time for 4.8 billion dollars. Meanwhile, the situation in South Vietnam continued to deteriorate both in terms of the military threat and political stability. The optimistic and extravagant claims of previous years had proved to be unfounded and counter-productive, and the bullish statements about the effect of the bombing raids again stimulated public scepticism – all the more so since Hanoi showed neither an inclination to discuss peace nor a significant lessening in its ability to wage war.

American forces were increasingly taking the offensive in Vietnam during the spring of 1966, but the administration was increasingly obliged to take defensive positions at home. With every new request for additional funds to meet the cost of the war, it was more difficult to satisfy members of Congress and a growing number of American people that the administration's policy was leading to either a political or a military solution.

In late October, the heads of government of the United States, South Vietnam, and the other countries with troops in Vietnam met in Manila. The two primary purposes of the Manila conference were to come to grips with the problems of a negotiated settlement and to project some lofty plans for the economic development of the Pacific area. In the event, the only specific proposal to emerge was an American commitment (grudgingly supported by the others) that United States forces would be withdrawn from Vietnam six months after it was determined that North Vietnamese forces had left. (Richard Nixon, with an eye on the next presidential contest, called the American offer a 'sell-out' of the South Vietnamese.) The North Vietnamese spurned the offer, however, and the war dragged on. During subsequent months, escalation of the ground and air wars would continue; more American troops would be deployed; casualties on both sides would increase and the war would exacerbate social, economic, and political problems at home.

American military commander General Westmoreland inspects a South Vietnamese River Defense Training Center near Saigon. The relationship between the US armed forces and their South Vietnamese ally was often strained.

3. From Rolling Thunder to the Tet Offensive

From 1965 to 1968, the US forces in Vietnam struggled to find an answer to the problems of fighting against the guerrillas of the Viet Cong. The overwhelming might of American airpower, was turned on the North during the *Rolling Thunder* series of operations, while ground troop levels were steadily built up to take on the communists in the countryside. The war was becoming a bitter battle of attrition, with casualty, tolls rising, when the Viet Cong launched a series of mass attacks on the urban centres of South Vietnam at the end of January 1968; and this so-called Tet offensive was to have far reaching consequences.

US troops take a rest during a search and destroy mission in the dense jungles around Xuan Loc.

Three years, all but one week, were to separate the first American bombing raid on North Vietnam and the start of the Tet Offensive. This period can be termed the American war because between 7 February 1965 and 31 January 1968 most aspects of the conflict in Indochina seemed to be dominated by the United States.

Even with the advantages of hindsight it is difficult to present a coherent picture of events in Indochina in these three years. The conflict assumed so many aspects, some of them contradictory, that the overall picture that emerges is one of bewildering complexity. In this period what had been until this time a war inside Indochina between states and within societies on this peninsula became internationalized, with the combat zone as much on the televisions, radios and in the newspapers of the world as in Indochina itself. It ceased to be a war fought for the most part inside South Vietnam between the South Vietnamese: the immediate theatre of operations became virtually the whole of Vietnam, North and South, with military forces from some 11 nations involved in just these two parts of Indochina. It was a period when the American military effort came to overshadow that of South Vietnam, yet throughout which South Vietnamese losses consistently and heavily outnumbered those of the Americans. It was a period when the Americans registered consistent success on the battlefield, yet the extent of that success was barely recognized at the time and was to come to a close with the event (the Tet Offensive) that was to prove, paradoxically, the most emphatic American–South Vietnamese military victory of the war and their gravest political defeat – from which there was to be no recovery. It was a period when it seemed that the USA and South Vietnam had been and would in future be dictating the course of the war, yet it ended with the realization that Hanoi, rather than Washington and Saigon, had largely shaped the pattern of events.

Above: Marine armoured vehicles combine with Marine infantry in an assault on NVA positions north of Dong Ha. The difficult terrain of most of South Vietnam meant that US armour played a relatively minor role. Right: General Westmoreland confers with US Defense Secretary Robert McNamara during a military briefing session in Saigon.

An uncertain commitment

Explanation of these various inconsistencies and contradictions is to be found in large measure in the nature of the American involvement in Vietnam. This involvement was a gradual one, the commitment not being made in any clear and decisive manner but over a period of time as the slow realization of the potentially disastrous situation inside South Vietnam dawned upon the administration of Lyndon B. Johnson. By definition this commitment was a faltering and uncertain one, and once made involved piecemeal deployment as the instinctive reaction to a lost strategic situation. Yet, for all this, the American commitment was to be made on such a scale and effectiveness by 1967 that by the end of that year the tide of war, running so firmly against South Vietnam in 1965, had been stemmed if not turned. The real tragedy of the American effort in Vietnam, and of South Vietnam in particular, was that success came too late to be exploited effectively. By the time that the Americans and South Vietnamese managed to work themselves into a potentially winning position, the cost of their past success prevented their being able to capitalize upon the advantage they gained after February 1968.

Just four words are crucial to any understanding of events between 1965 and 1968. These words relate to the state of affairs that confronted the Johnson administration after the elections of November 1964 had been fought and won. With the elections out of the way but with public concern growing about the state of affairs in Indochina, the Johnson administration, thus far cautious and restrained in its commitment of forces and support for South Vietnam, had to choose between abandoning and expanding its effort in Vietnam. This choice emerged because the administration came to realize that it faced *a lost strategic situation* in South Vietnam. At the end of 1964 and in the first months of 1965 it was realized that American power alone stood between the communists and victory, that there was no substitute for the reality of American might. By the end of 1964 the Johnson administration, advised by the Military Assistance Command Vietnam (MACV), had come to appreciate that the Army of the Republic of South Vietnam (ARVN) was losing and would continue to lose a conflict that was in the process of changing its character. By the end of 1964 the war in South Vietnam was changing from one that was being waged by small bands of indigenous South Vietnamese insurgents, the Viet Cong (VC), to one that was being prosecuted by an enemy beginning to operate in unit and formation strength. By 1965 a new phase of conventional warfare was clearly in the offing, and it was one to which North Vietnamese troops had been committed by Hanoi.

Corruption in South Vietnam

This was a war that the ARVN could not win. Demoralized by its losses and failure to deal with the VC, the ARVN lacked the strength to have any chance of meeting the direct threat posed by the North Vietnamese Army (as the Vietnamese People's Army had been renamed after 1954), while behind the 'front' the domestic situation within South Vietnam was scarcely less precarious. At the highest level Diem had yet to be replaced by a leader capable of uniting and rousing a

Top: The Americans wasted little time in bringing technology to bear in the conflict. In February 1965 an anti-aircraft battalion arrived at Da Nang air base equipped with Hawk missiles capable of destroying aircraft at a range of 45,000 feet (13,700m). Above: The communist anti-aircraft response was simpler – here a 37mm AA gun. Left: A Viet Cong guerrilla is shown making small-arms ammunition by hand.

Above: Resolute troops of the North Vietnamese Army move a gun barrel across rough terrain. Below: US Marines armed with M-14 rifles and pump-action shotguns move past Montagnard elephants on a patrol outside Khe Sanh in 1966.

divided and faction-ridden society, while at the lower levels administration had all but broken down. Corruption and stupefying apathy persisted at every level of the state bureaucracy and, critically, in many areas government itself had ceased to function. In some areas, indeed, government from Saigon had never existed, but even in those areas where it had there had developed a major crisis of confidence in Saigon's authority because of its manifest inability to protect the population from attack. In 1964 alone the VC killed or abducted over 11,200 people, more than 1500 of them government employees, from villages under ostensible government control. This, combined with the estimated 20,000 who had been killed or had disappeared in the previous six years, had the effect of destroying Saigon's credibility amongst the people whose support was critical to its very survival. In short, between 1960 and 1964 the VC, employing Giap's ploy of directing terrorism against the political infrastructure of the enemy, shattered the authority and prestige of Saigon throughout many areas of the countryside. In very sharp contrast to Malaya, where between 1948 and 1960 the British never had to contend with areas under undisputed enemy control, South Vietnamese anti-communist forces were to face the daunting prospects of establishing or re-establishing a discredited political infrastructure in the middle of a war that until 1965 or 1966 was clearly being lost.

It was against a background shaped by these various considerations that American policy evolved. Until 1964 the American interest in South Vietnam was political and moral, and its military commitment was relatively small. American determination to sustain South Vietnam had thus far taken the form of aid and advisers, but from this point on American policy was largely shaped by the calculation that with South Vietnam the target of communist aggression, the country had to be helped because failure to support her would only lead to further aggression elsewhere in the area. To the Johnson administration South Vietnam represented a *ne plus ultra* position where American credibility as a reliable ally would be demonstrated. To the Johnson administration the abandoning of an ally that had been encouraged and helped in its first ten years of life was unthinkable. Faced with having to decide between getting out of South Vietnam or becoming involved on a large scale, the decision in favour of the latter alternative was inevitable.

American military options

Initially, however, the scope of the American involvement was limited and mainly defensive since even the world's greatest power had its options limited by such considerations as time, distance and the availability of forces. In these circumstances it was perhaps unavoidable that the initial American commitment in 1965 should take the form of air power and the landing of Marines. The manner in which these deployments took place determined subsequent American policy to a large extent.

The deployment of American air power to the conflict represented one of the very few ways in which the Americans could immediately demonstrate their commitment to Saigon. It was a simple and effective option in the sense that the impact of air power was immediate and loss and damage would be inflicted on the enemy, but from the start the use of air power in Vietnam was a very vexed political, emotional and strategic issue.

The use of air power in this context meant the bombing of North Vietnam, contingency plans for such an eventuality having been made as early as March 1964. The strikes in August 1964 following the Gulf of Tonkin incident were represented as no more than a one-off retaliation, but by the turn of the year the MACV and the administration in Washington began to consider using American air power against the North for three reasons. Firstly, bombing the North would indicate American resolve to sustain South Vietnam. Secondly, it would serve to warn Hanoi of the American determination to make it pay for its aggression against the South. Thirdly, carrying the war to the otherwise invulnerable North was certain to calm clamour in Saigon (and America), to revive morale in the South and hopefully strengthen the incumbent regime in Saigon by putting an end to the interminable squabbles between the various military commanders. Bombing was seen as a means of rallying and uniting South Vietnam behind a genuinely popular cause.

To the Americans and South Vietnamese alike it was totally unacceptable that North Vietnam be allowed to direct the war in the South, and even to commit the North Vietnamese Army (NVA) to the battle, with impunity, remaining untouched by the consequences of her aggression. But how the North Vietnamese were to be made to pay for their aggression, and what the aim of any air offensive was to be, were problems that were not easy to solve. Essentially, the Americans had to decide between three courses of action: mounting small but punishing attacks in retaliation for specific enemy operations in the South; launching an all-out offensive from the start in an attempt to bomb North Vietnam back into the 'Stone Age' and thereby end the war by destroying its cause at source; mounting a slow but growing pressure

Right: Troops of the 101st Airborne Division repulse an enemy attack during Operation Hawthorne *in June 1966.*
Below: A US Air Force F-100 releases it bomb load on North Vietnamese positions north of Bien Hoa.

upon the North by a gradual but intensifying campaign.

Operation Rolling Thunder

The last option was the one that was to be adopted in the shape of *Rolling Thunder,* the bombing of the North between 2 March 1965 and 31 October 1968. Two reprisal operations, *Flaming Dart I* and *Flaming Dart II,* preceded the inauguration of *Rolling Thunder,* these two operations being mounted in retaliation for communist attacks on Pleiku on 7 February and Qui Nhon three days later. In both attacks American servicemen were killed and the subsequent air raids were portrayed as deliberate responses to these events. Yet the link between retaliation against specific communist attacks and a response to general communist aggression against the South was clearly so close that the distinction was certain to become blurred, and before the dust of Qui Nhon settled President Johnson had given approval for 'a program of measured and limited air action . . . against military targets [in North Vietnam].'

From the start bombing was both politically and militarily controversial. At the beginning *Rolling Thunder* was seen as an attempt to punish North Vietnam for its aggression, but this simple and instinctive urge was very quickly reversed in favour of the deliberate attempt to exert pressure on Hanoi. It was intended to induce the communists to come to terms by convincing them that the war could not be won and that any attempt to persist in aggression would

Opposite above: A US F-4 Phantom fires its rockets in support of American ground-force operations. Opposite below: Phantoms take on fuel from a KC-135 tanker before going on to bomb a target in North Vietnam.
Above: North Vietnamese interceptor pilots undergo briefing. Below right: A US helicopter gunner scans the marshland of the Mekong Delta for signs of enemy activity.

result in unacceptable damage being inflicted upon the North. In this context the slow and deliberate increase in pressure, the 'slow squeeze' approach that saw an escalation of bombing or its moderation in response to Hanoi's own actions, was conceived as a rational and very deliberate political act, the application of an appropriate level of force in pursuit of the objective which was to secure negotiations and an end to the war. By exercising restraint at the outset the Johnson administration left itself with the choice of if and when to escalate or to impose pauses in the course of operations. By exercising such restraint Washington believed that the possibilities of Chinese intervention and a dangerous widening of the conflict would be minimized. Moreover, the gradualist approach would enable the Americans and South Vietnamese to play the role of the injured parties displaying moderation in the face of the North's aggression.

Hanoi's diplomatic victory

The Americans were determined to pursue the bombing option in parallel with the diplomatic option, yet the assumption that bombing was something that the Americans could moderate or intensify because theirs was the power of decision was not correct – as events quickly revealed. Though behind-the-scenes contacts between Hanoi and Washington were maintained throughout the period, in public Hanoi represented bombing as the obstacle to negotiations. Moreover, by a masterly publicity campaign of blatant misrepresentation Hanoi portrayed the bombing of the North as a deliberate attempt on the part of the Americans to exterminate a small, defenceless and inoffensive country that was forced to fight in order to defend itself against aggressive Yankee imperialism.

Had North Vietnam been what it claimed to be there would have been no Vietnam war in the first place, but such was the subtlety of the misinformation peddled by Hanoi and its fellow-travellers in the West that the picture of a benign and pacific North Vietnam, assailed by the mightiest military machine on earth, was one that gained widespread acceptance in the outside world. Though the Johnson administration was correct in its assessment of Hanoi's leadership as a bunch of ruthless hard-line communists who respected nothing but superior force, Hanoi's manipulation and orchestration of the media cast the USA in the role of the aggressor and bully and North Vietnam as the victim. Washington was correct in its view that bombing would not prove an obstacle to negotiations, but that was not how bombing came to be regarded. Instead it very quickly became a crippling political liability.

The concept of the 'slow squeeze' also had its opponents within South Vietnam, the American military and the administration because it was widely felt that the various restraints imposed on *Rolling Thunder* reduced its effectiveness and served to prevent it ever realizing its objectives. The proponents of the 'all-out' offensive, made with full strength against any target in North Vietnam, had little confidence in a policy of restraint ever forcing Hanoi to come to terms, and chafed at the pauses periodically imposed on *Rolling Thunder*. The most important of these temporary halts (13–18 May 1965, 24 December 1965–31 January 1966 and 15 January–10 February 1968) were regarded as dangerous since they gave the North Vietnamese respites; as futile since the enemy never showed the

Top: A B-52 bomber drops 1000 and 750 lb (340 and 450 kg) bombs on targets in North Vietnam. Above: A North Vietnamese SA-2 Guideline Surface-to-Air Missile (SAM) is prepared for action. Guided by radar this was the most sophisticated weapon in the communist air defence system. Left: Fearful of direct US action against North Vietnam, communist soldiers place mines on a beach near Dong Hoi.

least sign of exercising corresponding self-restraint or a change of heart; as damaging on the grounds that they weakened rather than strengthened American credibility.

Smashing the communists?

The arguments over political aims and strategic objectives plagued *Rolling Thunder* which throughout its existence was never more than a compromise between these conflicting views within the American command. The inevitable compromise was to prevent the realization of both the political and the strategic objectives of the entire operation. This state of affairs was recognized by Defense Secretary Robert McNamara in October 1966 when he advised Johnson that bombing had failed to make much impact on the flow of men and materials from the North to the South. In fact the flow had increased, despite the fact that in 1966 the number of missions flown against the North nearly tripled over the previous year from 55,000 to 148,000. With B-52 bombers joining the offensive after 12 April 1966, the tonnage of bombs dropped on North Vietnam almost quadrupled, but the fact of the matter was that the American leadership had underestimated North Vietnam's willingness and ability to absorb punishment.

The majority of the attacks were concentrated in the panhandle, away from the few industrial centres in the country, and even the operations against North Vietnam's communications system had little real effect. The system in fact expanded and diversified under air attack, and losses of road and rail transport were made good from China and Soviet bloc countries. Similarly the attacks on the North's oil installations resulted in effective dispersal. The cost to the North was heavy, but with weather preventing continuous operations and the Americans refraining from striking at the two targets whose destruction could have paralysed the North's economy (Haiphong harbour and the Red River dykes), there could be no question of *Rolling Thunder* proving capable of crippling a society whose very backwardness was an

Above: Huge craters caused by 750 lb (340 kg) bombs litter the highway beside the Kim Kuong bridge, now in ruins after an American air strike. Below: Despite the destruction the Ho Chi Minh Trail remained in operation. Below right: Combined air and fire-support-base operations were highly effective in disrupting communist attacks.

asset. By December 1967 a total of 864,000 tons of bombs had been dropped on North Vietnam (over 50 per cent more than the total dropped by all sides in the course of the Pacific War of 1941–45) yet by that time there was no sign of any weakening of Hanoi's determination or capacity to continue the war, and, indeed, between January and October 1968 the number of men sent to the South exceeded the total sent in the previous three years (about 230,000 compared to 220,000). Far from forcing Hanoi to modify its behaviour, bombing of the North had no immediate or perceptible impact on North Vietnam's determination and ability to continue the war.

What bombing did, however, was to reduce the level of infiltration from what it would have been had there been no *Rolling Thunder*. This was the view of the overall commander of the American effort, Admiral U.S.G. Sharp, Commander-in-Chief of the Pacific Fleet. This is a somewhat contentious view, but it is a convenient one because it leads to the question of the American commitment of combat troops to South Vietnam in 1965 and the strategy employed by the American command in Vietnam between 1965 and 1968. Moreover, Sharp's view is one that is vitally important because it assumes a direct relationship between the level of infiltration from the North and the level of insurgency in the South. There is no doubt that such a relationship existed, but the question of which was the dependent factor is not easy to discern.

The general view at the time was that the gradual change of fortune in the South meant that by 1968 the momentum of the war was only being maintained by Hanoi's commitment of the NVA to the struggle, that the level of insurgency within South Vietnam was dependent on the force levels dispatched by Hanoi. Yet the determinant of the level of effective infiltration from the North in the final analysis could not be the supply and manpower capacity of the North but the capacity of insurgency within the South to absorb outside support. Had South Vietnam been pacified no amount of infiltration from the North could have proved effective because it could not have been accommodated, the inevitable consequence of such a situation being that Hanoi would have been forced either to employ conventional tactics or abandon its attempt to subjugate the South.

American doubts

This is no mere academic exercise in semantics because this chicken-and-egg situation lay at the heart of the problem

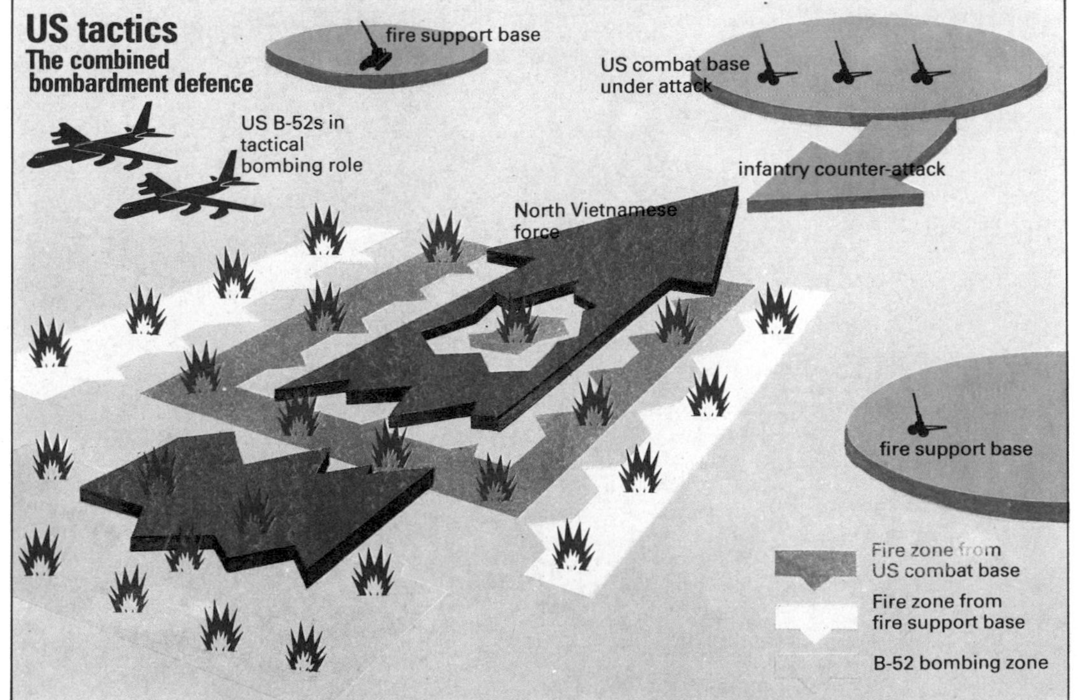

Above: A battery of 7.62mm mini-guns mounted on a converted AC-47 open fire on a suspected target. Capable of firing several thousand rounds per minute the mini-gun was a devastating weapon when used against soft targets. Left: A US Marine machine-gun team comes under fire during an attack on a Viet Cong position. Below: South Vietnamese Rangers prepare to fire a recoilless rifle on a search and destroy operation near Da Nang. The Rangers were considered to be among the best troops in the ARVN.

of trying to formulate a coherent strategic doctrine within South Vietnam between 1965 and 1968. The situation that confronted the Americans at the time of the instigation of *Rolling Thunder* was critical since the war, as we have already seen, was then on the point of transformation from a guerrilla struggle to one that combined guerrilla and open conventional warfare. In those first weeks of 1965 MACV became increasingly pessimistic about the prospects confronting the ARVN. It believed that bombing the North could not make any impact on events in the South for at least six months, and that it would take at least one year to expand the size and improve the quality of the ARVN to the point where it could deal with the VC alone.

The logic of the military situation was inescapable. Though *Rolling Thunder* had been seen as a possible means of avoiding a commitment of substantial ground forces to South Vietnam, such a commitment could not be avoided because there was no possibility of the ARVN being able to deal with the VC and at the same time face the NVA. Only the Americans could counter the emerging threat posed by the NVA, and this could only be done if the Americans committed forces on a large scale to the South. But just as the example of the Korean War and fear of Chinese intervention cast long shadows over the conduct of *Rolling Thunder,* so such a commitment was certain to raise political and moral issues within the United States. This very issue was to be the critical aspect of the struggle between 1965 and 1968 because in making its commitment to the South in 1965 the Johnson administration made its most serious error of judgment of the war. Just as it was mistaken in its belief that it and not Hanoi held the power of decision with regard to the bombing of the North, so it assumed that it could determine the nature of the ground war in South Vietnam. In making this assumption it failed to appreciate the true nature of the war and Hanoi's real intentions, and it tried to make the war into something that it was not and could not be.

The Marines arrive

At the outset the American commitment of ground troops was tentative, defensive and limited in scope. President Johnson's approval of the deployment of Marines to Da Nang on 26 February 1965 was the first step in what was the 'enclave strategy' whereby the Americans sought to protect their own bases, particularly their air bases, from communist attack. Thus the 9th Marine Expeditionary Brigade came ashore on 8 March in order to provide for the local defence of Da Nang as part of a strategy that was unwanted by MACV and which was doomed to failure. A policy of local and passive defence had no future in a war where there was no 'front'. The Marines had to be drawn into an ever-widening commitment around their own bases (the start of the 'credibility gap') and this became the first step in a much more significant widening of American strategic policy as the Americans accepted the need for their concentration against the NVA. As American policy evolved, its main themes were that the Americans should tackle the enemy's main forces by moving into the disputed areas while the ARVN was left free to concentrate on the twin tasks of pacifying the countryside and building up its strength.

This division of responsibilities was sensible in that it left the task of dealing with the VC in the hands of those best suited to do it, namely the indigenous population. It also left the Americans free to fight the type of war they understood, main-force battle. Given strategic doctrine that over the past hundred years had stressed firepower, mass, speed and shock action to secure overwhelming superiority at the point of battle and thereby impose one's own will on the enemy, the American preoccupation with battle, plus their confidence that they would win, was both natural and understandable. Given the prevailing situation inside South Vietnam Westmoreland's much reviled observation, 'The answer to insurgency is firepower,' was not as stupid and unimaginative as has been suggested. for given the commitment of the NVA to battle, firepower had to be at least a major part of the answer to the problem of defending South Vietnam, and without it Saigon would have gone under in 1965.

Above: US Marines engage in a desultory fire-fight against the Viet Cong in the highland region of South Vietnam just south of Khe Sanh. Right: Armed with an M-16 rifle a US infantry scout prepares to engage the enemy. Below right: A River Patrol Boat (PBR) at full speed near Cat Lo in South Vietnam. Vessels such as this formed the basis for the riverine warfare force which was responsible for protecting the Mekong Delta region against the VC.

Where Westmoreland, and by extension Washington, was wrong was partly in the assessment of the force levels needed to provide the answer that was to be imposed on Hanoi. Westmoreland's assessment was for a total of 275,000 troops to halt the deterioration of the situation within South Vietnam by the end of 1965 and to build up sufficient reserves to allow major offensive action in the course of the following year. This request was approved on 28 July 1965, and by the end of the year 184,300 American servicemen were in South Vietnam. But the combat element of three divisions and

four regiments was inadequate to deal with the growing challenge posed by a Hanoi that chose to escalate its own commitment as part of a deliberate attempt to wage protracted warfare.

Hanoi's strategy of attrition

It was here that the Americans made their most important error. They underestimated the force levels they needed and they underrated the physical difficulties that confronted them within Indochina, but far more important was the fact that they failed to appreciate that Hanoi did not regard war and battle in the same light as they did. Hanoi, working to the concepts of Mao Tse-tung with modifications provided by Giap and Ho Chi Minh, saw war as a political phenomenon in which psychological and ideological factors and not military considerations were the decisive elements. According to the Hanoi formula of war, military effectiveness was dependent on the level of political commitment, and in the pursuit of victory Hanoi sought to mobilize opinion (both internationally in order to bring pressure on the Americans and internally in order to make the population sustain a war effort) and to exploit time and space in order to wear down American resolve and resources. Hanoi sought not to win battles but to prolong the war

Above: A wounded US Marine is comforted by a chaplain while awaiting evacuation from the battle-zone. Right: The growing level of American involvement in Vietnam during the sixties was expressed by a steady increase in manpower. As the numbers increased so too did the casualties, which, in the end, led to public disenchantment with the war.

by denying the Americans any tactical success that might prove strategically decisive, and the means by which it sought to do this, the coin in which the bills of time, space and will had to be paid, was the sacrifice of lives. This was a price that Hanoi was willing to pay. With no restraints on its treatment of its population and with no need to accept the self-imposed burden of international and domestic opinion that weighed down the United States, Hanoi sought to draw out the struggle to the point where the American administration would be unable to sustain its effort. And it was the pursuit of this policy that won the North the war.

Below: A US soldier hurls a grenade while supported by covering fire from a comrade armed with an M-16 rifle. Bottom: A badly wounded US Marine is led to a waiting Medevac helicopter.

Vietnamese predictions

In an interview granted to *The Australian* in 1965 Ho Chi Minh stated that within a couple of years American cities would become centres of turmoil and strife until the time came when the American attempt to sustain South Vietnam was abandoned. After the election results of November 1964 and with American expectations aroused by Johnson's vision of 'The Great Society', this prediction seemed at the time to be preposterous, yet it was one that was borne out. Though many factors were to be involved in producing the American domestic crisis of the late sixties (particularly 1968), Vietnam was to be the most important single cause as Hanoi deliberately set about sapping American determination by an insidious propaganda campaign aimed at the American population. In exactly the same way as France had been undermined by communist propaganda in the course of the earlier struggle in Indochina, so the communists set about spreading defeatism, fatalism, apathy and scepticism in constituted authority amongst a population traditionally reared on quick results.

Quick results were beyond the Americans in Vietnam. Disastrous as this situation was, it was exacerbated by an ever-growing deployment that peaked in January 1969 with 542,000 servicemen in South Vietnam. Yet even with the support of other Free-World countries that by 1968 contributed 65,800 troops to the effort in South Vietnam, the Americans were to find the realization of their objectives tantalizingly elusive. This elusiveness was to prove far more significant than the very real triumphs that were recorded on the battlefield.

In the years 1965–68, the Americans achieved four major successes. Firstly, they worsted the VC and NVA in a manner that had earlier been beyond the capacity of the ARVN, and in part the increasing flow of men and materials from the North reflected the losses suffered by the communists as the Americans bit into their operational strength. Secondly, the Americans brought a large measure of security to their main base areas, though the net around their bases could never be made proof against small but costly, well-planned and well-executed communist attacks. Thirdly, the Americans fought their way up through the A Shau, A Luoi, An Lao, An Tuc and Que Son river valleys which provided the North with five of its most important infiltration routes into the South. Fourthly, the Americans took the war into the Central Highlands. This latter area had been perhaps the most immediate concern of MACV in the early months of 1965 because any communist conventional offensive erupting out of the Central Highlands was certain to split South Vietnam in two. This possibility was ended by the Americans, though the events of 1975 were to show just how real and disastrous such an offensive would be. In the north, in the Central Highlands, and in War Zones C and D near Saigon, the Americans were successful in taking the war into areas that had been totally or very largely dominated by the VC for at least a decade.

These were very real successes, but compared to the expectations and demands of the American public they were failures. At best these successes were disappointments, and in any event they were really no more than partial successes since some of the areas that were the scene of American drives against the communists had to be fought for time and again because of the main shortcoming of the American effort. On all too many occasions the Americans lacked the means of consolidating success. Though American operational boundaries corresponded to those of the ARVN, the latter was all too often incapable of moving into an area and securing it. With a police force that was not even placed on a war footing in this period, there was no means by which Saigon could deploy its agencies into areas from which the enemy had been temporarily driven. The result was that the VC were like the tide in that they flowed back once the war had passed by.

ARVN in trouble

The weakness of the ARVN was certainly one of the most important factors in explaining why the anti-communist forces were never able to capitalize on the success that came their way, but it was not the only factor and perhaps it was not even the most important one. The police were weak; the administration as a whole was inefficient and of poor quality; the plethora of intelligence agencies working in South Vietnam were not properly co-ordinated and controlled. But the fact of the matter was that even though the ARVN grew from 250,000 in 1964 to 343,000 in 1967 and to 427,000 in 1968 and thence to 493,000 in the course of the following year, it was never able to meet the demands imposed by having to fight a war that was prosecuted over a wide surface area. In effect, the ARVN was forced to operate with force levels that were really five years behind its operational needs. Even with a 50 per cent growth in the size of auxiliary and local defence forces to a total of 393,000 men and women between 1964 and 1968, the ARVN was too stretched to be able to stand against an enemy with the options of when, where and how to mount its offensive operations. It was a problem shared by the Americans since even with their numbers they had immense difficulties in raising a full division's worth of troops for offensive operations. To concentrate 20,000 troops for combat required a major effort that could only be made by stripping 'quiet' sectors that were, as often as not, infiltrated by the NVA and VC as soon as they were evacuated by their previous occupiers. In such a situation of uncertainty it was small wonder that relatively few South Vietnamese in disputed areas committed themselves fully to Saigon since there was no guarantee that they would be protected against the inevitable atrocities that the communists perpetrated in areas that they recovered.

The root of the ARVN-American problems lay in the fact that their basic weakness of numbers left them with an insoluble number-to-space conundrum that was exaggerated by the fact that South Vietnam had a 900-mile (1450 km) border with her neighbours that could be infiltrated for much of its length. It was impossible to control the border yet it was clearly desirable that it should be closed. In Cambodia and Laos the communists had sanctuaries and infiltration routes that left them in a position to

Above: Two US Marines catch some sleep in the rain and mud of a trench line at Lon Thien. Left: Large stocks of French 9mm MAT sub-machine guns were captured from the French by the North Vietnamese and were still in use in the sixties. Particular features of the weapon were the sliding metal stock and the swing-operation magazine, shown here folded away against the barrel. Below left: A wounded ARVN soldier in unceremoniously carried to a field dressing station. Despite US aid South Vietnamese resources were not always of the first order. Above right: A US Marine is treated for wounds during the fighting for Hué in the Tet Offensive. Right: Yellow smoke flares are set off by men of the 173rd Airborne Brigade signalling their capture of a hilltop in the mountainous area around Dak To.

Above: Supplies are dropped by parachute to the beleaguered firebase of Khe Sanh in northern South Vietnam in March 1968. Left: A firebase mortar in action. Below: The crew of a US Navy monitor take a rest during operations on the Mekong River.

determine the timing, tempo and direction of their efforts with little that the ARVN and the Americans could do to oppose them.

Ultimately the Americans were to build some 50 firebases along the border, the most important of them being collectively known as the McNamara Line, to the south of the supposedly Demilitarized Zone (DMZ) that separated the two Vietnams. This Line was a series of bases so located as to prevent or at least hinder communist infiltration across the shortest and most direct route from the North to the South. These bases, the most famous of which were Khe Sanh and Con Thien, were linked by various obstacles and sensors that were intended to cut down enemy activity in and across the DMZ which began in 1966 but which only assumed serious proportions in the opening months of 1967.

The firebase controversy

The firebase concept was not popular with MACV because Westmoreland's command was very conscious that such bases made inordinately heavy demands on very scarce infantry resources yet were relatively ineffective. The notion of obstacles between firebases could only be made real by the deployment of infantry to make them effective, and along the western frontier firebases could not hope to prove effective because of the distance between them and the general reluctance of American forces to get into the jungle for sustained periods. With the mobility of helicopters at their disposal, American forces proved notoriously unwilling to commit themselves to long-range patrolling on the ground. But the McNamara Line was established because of the fear that unless steps were taken to seal off the southern exits from the DMZ the North Vietnamese might prove capable of securing the two northern provinces of South Vietnam, after which they might seek to negotiate. Thus the Americans found themselves after late 1966 committed to a policy of trying to control the western border and to seal the northern frontier with insufficient troops who were in any event wary of patrolling the terrain except by helicopter.

These numerical and tactical weaknesses were to have one very important repercussion. In the course of 1967, even while American forces registered some very important successes, support for the Vietnam commitment very slowly began to come apart within American society. Several factors were involved in this process, but one of the more important was the fact that the lack of combat strength and forces on the ground meant that the Americans relied on artillery and air power to win battles. In areas that were very often heavily populated, the consequences for the local South Vietnamese civilians were frequently disastrous. Undoubtedly the reliance on air power and artillery saved very many American lives, but the all-too-frequent consequences of such a tactical doctrine had damaging political consequences.

Americans against the war

The Vietnam War was the first 'television war', with napalm and shell fire on the breakfast menu. For a society that in any case retained genuine doubts about the morality and wisdom of the course of action on which the Johnson administration was embarked, the revelation of the brutality of war had a devastating impact, especially when policy statements in 1967 seemed to indicate not a short-term commitment but a long haul in Vietnam. The continuous upward adjustments of required force levels were always accompanied by optimistic assessments of the situation, but in April Westmoreland presented President Johnson with alternative requests, that the Americans commit a 'minimum essential force' of 550,000 men that would enable the United States to liquidate its commitment to South Vietnam in five years, or that the administration sanction the establishment of an 'optimum force' of 670,000 men that would achieve the same result in three years.

Under mounting political pressure, Johnson temporized with the promise of 520,000 men, less than Westmoreland's minimum requirement. Under the circumstances Westmoreland was more or less ordered to complete his mission with what he had rather than with what he wanted, but this obviously unsatisfactory state of affairs did not prevent Westmoreland from predicting on 21 November in a speech that was soon to become notorious that 'We have reached an important point when the end begins to come into view.'

The prediction was to be very quickly borne out by events, but not quite in the manner that Westmoreland intended. But light at the end of the tunnel by this stage had been dangled in front of the American public so often that a not unnatural scepticism greeted a military optimism that had always gone hand-in-hand with requests for more troops. What made this particular situation of late 1967 so very different was not so much that it came after earlier discredited requests but that it coincided with a very marked anti-war upsurge within the United States, and it was to be followed by an event that shattered the credibility not simply of Westmoreland but of the John-

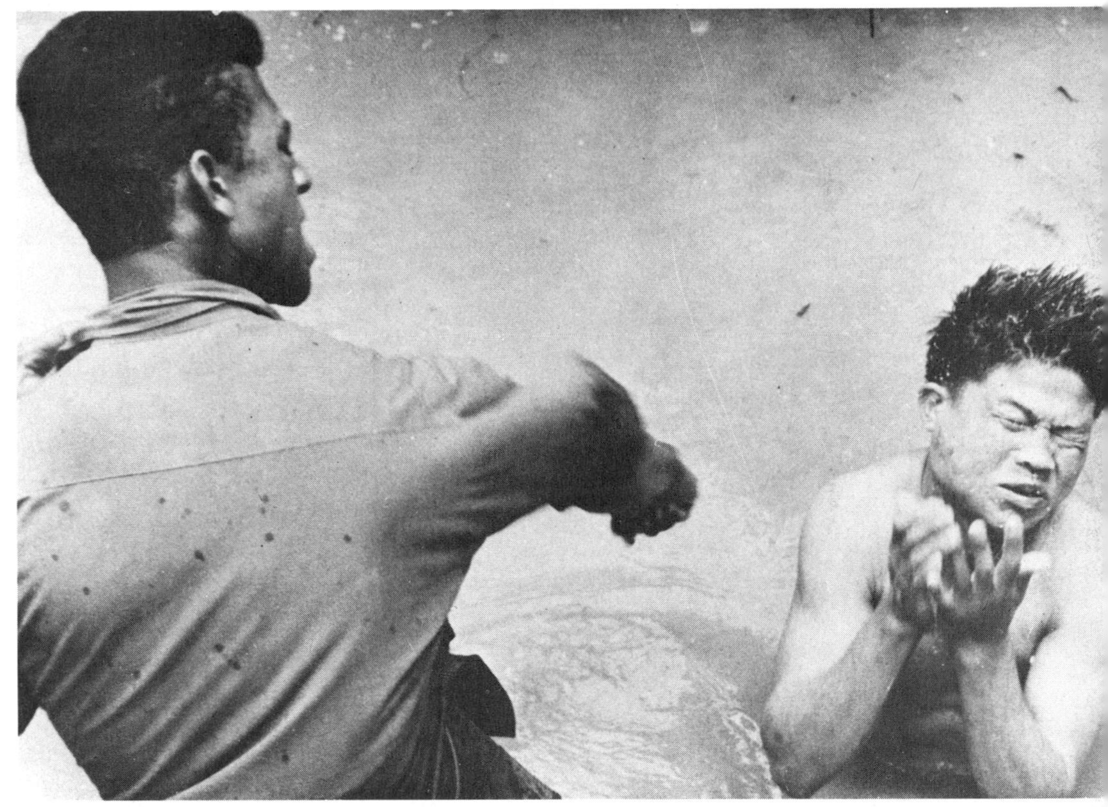

Right: US troops survey a knocked-out North Vietnamese 122mm howitzer that had, until recently, been firing upon them. Below: A captured Viet Cong soldier undergoes rigorous interrogation from his American captor. The nature of the war ensured that the rules of the Geneva Convention were so blurred as to be unrecognizable at times.

Left: Heavily-laden North Vietnamese troops trudge along a country road. The armament carried includes the Chinese Type 56-1 assault rifle – a cut-down version of the Soviet AK-47, complete with folding metal stock. Below left: North Vietnamese volunteers receive instruction in a woodside clearing. The 'blackboard' cut into the tree is bomb-shaped, a possible reflection of the heavy bombing endured by the North Vietnamese.

son administration.

This crisis came about as a result of another and earlier crisis that had occurred, not, for once, in South Vietnam but in Hanoi. The communist leadership in North Vietnam by the end of 1967 was in a position not dissimilar to that of the Johnson administration since both, for the first time, were beginning to have doubts about their capacity to last the course. It was not that the communists had any second thoughts about their ultimate aim, the destruction of South Vietnam and the subjugation of the whole of Indochina to their rule, but by the second half of the year it was becoming clear that the price of victory was going to be far higher than had been expected and, more critically, that events in the South were no longer working to the advantage of the communist leadership in Hanoi.

The political infighting inside Saigon had been largely stilled. Buddhist protests and self-immolation were fading into the background as South Vietnam, under constant American proddings, began to organize itself and create some sort of political order despite the war. In September the South's strong man, General Nguyen Van Thieu, was installed as president after an election generally regarded as honest and fair. Equally, the military situation did not seem to hold out much hope for Hanoi. However willing North Vietnam had been to accept losses in an effort to wear down American resolve, by mid-1967 communist losses were beginning for the first time to assume serious proportions.

By 1967 the North was having to send 10,000 troops to the South every month simply in order to maintain its operations, and this was not far short of the total number sent to the South in the whole of 1964. Yet despite this effort the communists in 1967 controlled less area and fewer people than had been under their rule three years earlier. Moreover, the period 1964–7 was one when the communists needed to expand their forces on a massive scale if there was to be any realistic prospect of their securing victory in the long term, and this was not achieved. It was remarkable that between December 1964 and December 1967 the communist main forces in the South increased in size by almost 50 per cent (from about 180,000 to 260,000) despite losses of perhaps 330,000 troops. The communists were able to deny the Americans the moment when communist losses exceeded their replacement capacity, yet by 1967 it was clear that such a time could not be delayed for much longer. With ever more resources being committed to the defence of North Vietnam itself, the communist leadership knew that things could not go on as they were. The VC and NVA could not go on indefinitely suffering the sort of reverses that they incurred in early 1967. In Operation *Cedar Falls* in January the Americans and ARVN had effectively destroyed the communist sanctuary known as the Iron Triangle some 20 miles (32 km) north of Saigon itself: in Operation *Junction City*, carried out between February and May, the communists had suffered a bad but not irreversible defeat in War Zone C. The communists had also suffered defeats in front of Khe Sanh, Gio Linh and Con Thien on the McNamara Line as part of *Hickory*, while Operations *Malheur* and *Dragon Head* (conducted by South Korean troops) did much to destroy the communist position in Quang Ngai. Clearly, by the second half of 1967 the omens were hardly auspicious for Hanoi.

Planning the Tet Offensive

Under these circumstances in July 1967 Hanoi ordered its forces to prepare for an all-out offensive in the South. This reversal of tactics was agreed upon only after acrimonious debate within the Central Committee, and it would appear that many members of the communist hierarchy had little confidence in a plan that envisaged an offensive throughout South Vietnam made with all available forces at the time of the Lunar New Year festivities (Tet) in 1968. This offensive was supposedly designed to achieve three objectives: to provoke a general uprising in the South that would sweep all before it; to shatter the ARVN; to destroy the Americans' political and military positions in the South.

There was some lack of clarity about these objectives since they are obviously not wholly compatible, but the real weakness of the intention was that it was compromised in the course of American operations in the Central Highlands in late 1967. Information later supplied by prisoners and deserters confirmed that supplied from captured documents, the Americans and ARVN thus being forewarned of the enemy's intentions before one of the main diversionary efforts began on 21 January 1968 with an attack on the Khe Sanh firebase. This offensive, conducted by an estimated two NVA divisions, was to outlive the main effort, perhaps because after the collapse of the Tet Offensive Hanoi sought a success against Khe Sanh's American defenders

Top: A US Navy PACV (Patrol Air Cushion Vehicle) crosses a rice paddy while on patrol in the low-lying areas south-west of Saigon. Above: An anti-aircraft unit of the NVA crosses a repaired bridge in North Vietnam. This unit was part of the elite Song Gienh force which claimed to have shot down 162 US aircraft and contributed to the downing of a further 80.

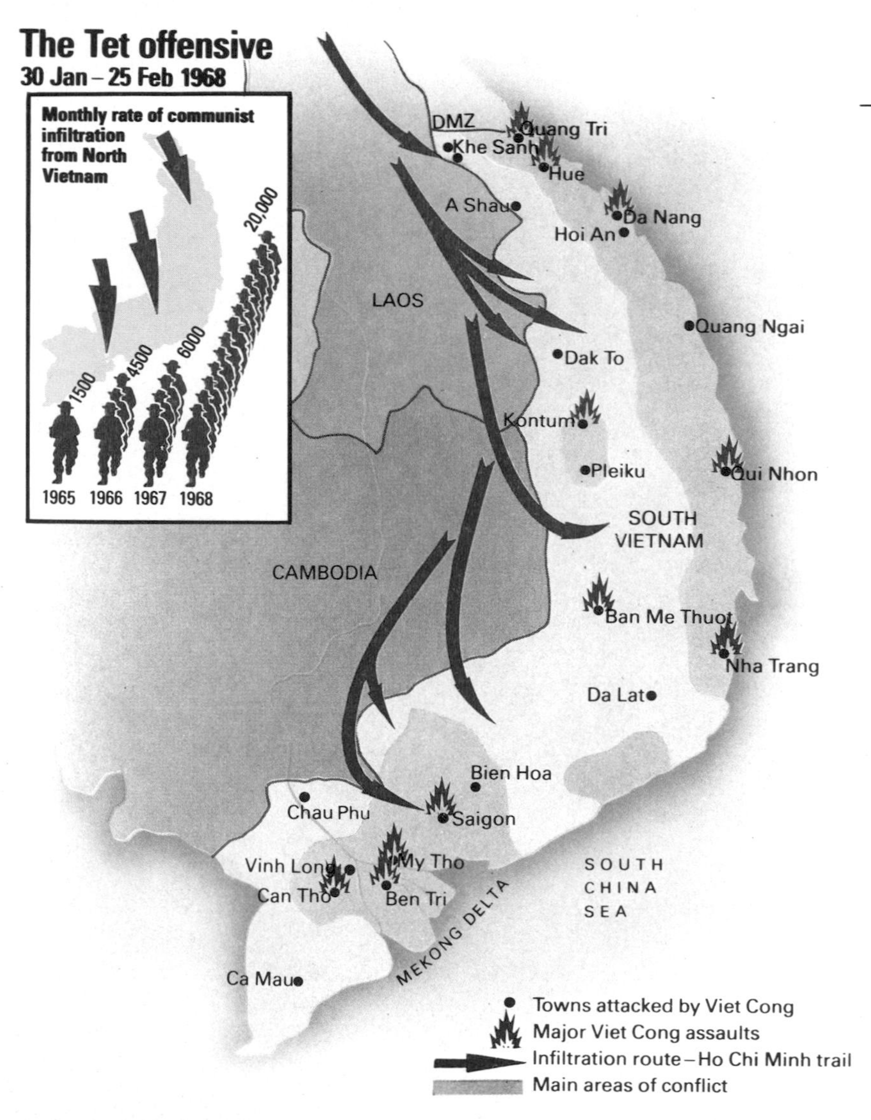

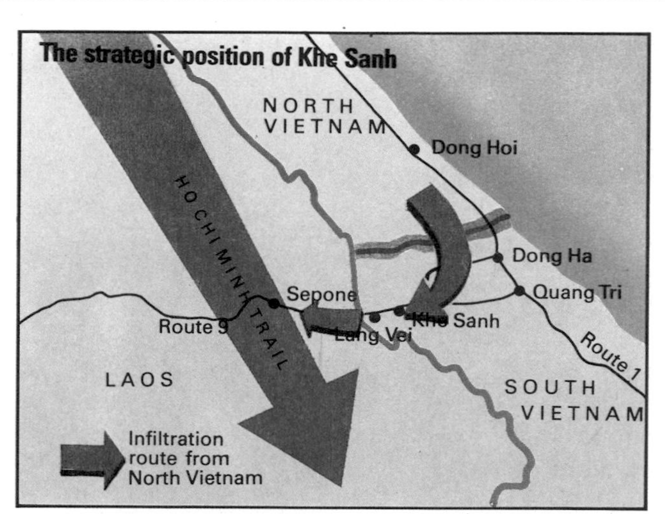

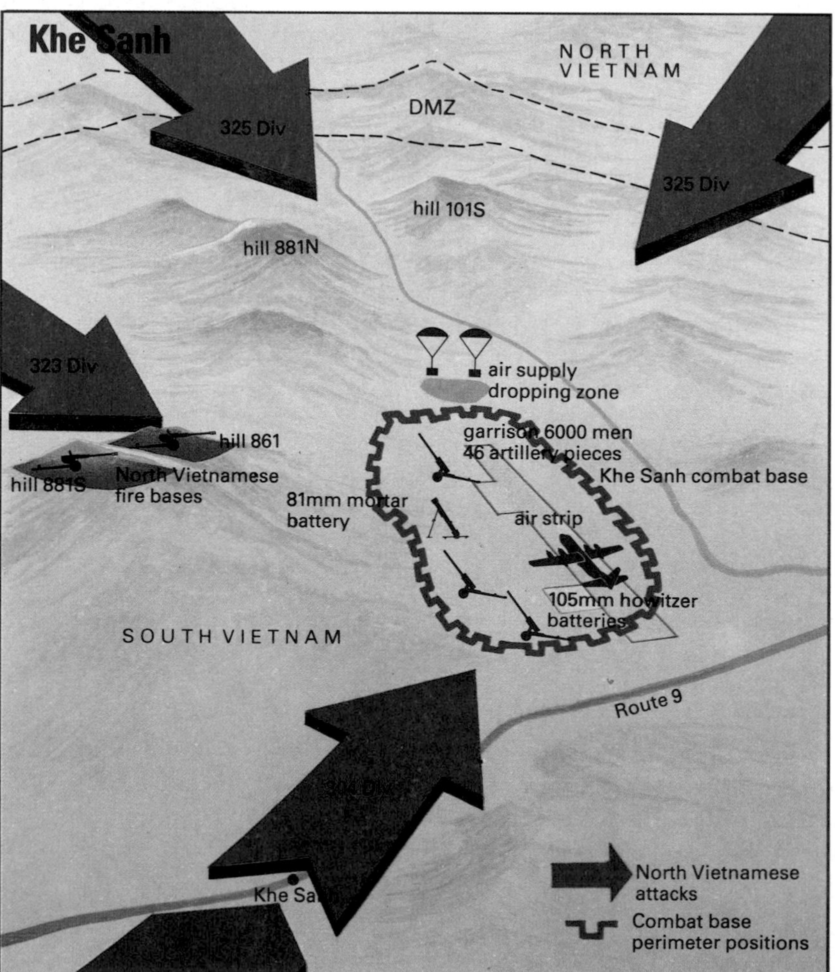

Above left: The Tet Offensive came as surprise to the US armed forces and had far-reaching political consequences. Top: The communist attack on Khe Sanh was the major ground battle of the Tet Offensive. Above: US Marine tank crews observe the results of American air support on the Khe Sanh perimeter. Left: Khe Sanh – the tactical situation. Although outnumbered the US Marines at Khe Sanh could rely on massive and accurate air support.
Opposite above: A helicopter prepares to airlift Marines from the besieged base. Opposite below: US Marines shelter from sniper fire behind an M48 medium tank during the bitter fighting in Hué.

that would compensate for the failure of the wider endeavour. The siege of Khe Sanh was not to be partially lifted until 6 April, and the base was not finally relieved until 14 April.

During the time that the position was under attack there were many gloomy predictions that Khe Sanh would prove to be America's Dien Bien Phu. But while the situation was often critical, the effectiveness of American air power was such that Westmoreland's assessment that Khe Sanh could and should be defended and that it could and would withstand assault was shown to be correct. In the first four weeks of the siege 60,000 tons of napalm were dropped around Khe Sanh, and in the entire operation more than 100,000 tons of bombs were aimed at the communist positions around the base. As the besiegers' grip was broken it was suggested by some Western commentators that the NVA never intended to take Khe Sanh but were intent on tying down American combat formations in its defence. By such logic defeats are turned into victories, yet two aspects were clear about the Khe Sanh episode by the end of March. Firstly, the defence of the base did indeed tie down a very considerable part of American combat strength. The actual garrison was about 6000 troops, but some 15,000 more combat troops, and a large part of the American air effort, had to be directed to the general defence of the base. Secondly, by March there was no overwhelming need to take the base as far as the NVA was concerned: Tet had done its work.

This offensive opened prematurely on 30 January when communist forces attacked eight cities and towns in the Central Highlands and in the central coastal plain. The main attacks were made the following day. Overall the 70,000 (plus) VC and NVA troops committed to these operations attacked 36 of the country's 44 provincial capitals, 64 of the 242 district capitals and five of South Vietnam's six autonomous cities. These attacks were supposed to be very different from the type of small sabotage or terrorist operations (or mortar and artillery bombardments) thus far employed by the communists in their urban forays. In this offensive the communists tried to fight their way into and then hold cities and towns, partly in order to set off the anticipated popular uprising and partly to ensure that opposition elements were eliminated. What this latter phenomenon meant became grimly apparent after the liberation of the old imperial capital of Hué, one of the two cities that alone saw prolonged fighting during Tet.

In previous times the VC had been very selective in its choice of targets and had employed a formidable array of ghastly techniques of torture, mutilation and death (impaling, crucifixion, burying alive, progressive amputation, mutilation of body orifices and emasculation) in order to cow potential enemies. At Hué, however, the communists set about the deliberate murder of entire family units – women, children, babies, servants, pet animals and birds. In various places victims were buried to their waists and then sliced open, shoulders and arms remaining as upright Vees for the fallen head, throat and upper chest. At Hué alone, where the communists were not eliminated until 25 February, more than 1000 bodies were recovered from mass graves, and at least five times that number were murdered nationwide by the VC and NVA in the course of the Tet Offensive. At least 12,000 civilians were killed in the crossfire as battle was joined, the ARVN and Americans between them eliminating all opposition except in Saigon and Hué within two or three days.

The Tet Offensive manifestly failed in two of its aims. It failed to break the ARVN on whom the brunt of the fighting fell. The ARVN suffered 11,674 casualties of whom 8299 were wounded (the Americans and the other allies lost 1547 killed and missing and 7764 wounded) but it fought well and its success naturally strengthened its self-confidence. Voluntary enlistment increased in the months after Tet. The offensive also failed to provoke a general uprising. In reality there was never any chance of such a rising. If one did not take place in 1964

when Saigon was discredited, the ARVN was in disarray and the Americans not in sufficient force to be effective, then one was not going to take place in 1968. The absence of any form of popular uprising between 1960 and 1975 revealed the hollowness of the communist claim to be a popular movement, a point that American critics consistently ignore.

But if Tet had two failures it also had three losers. Firstly, upwards of 750,000 civilians were made homeless during Tet, and many others lost their possessions during the widespread damage done to many cities and towns in the South. It was the devastation wrought at Ben Tre that gave rise to one of the most famous comments of the war, that 'it became necessary to destroy the town to save it'. Secondly, the VC was destroyed as an effective force. After Tet the war was fought by the NVA since the VC had virtually ceased to exist. Estimates of NVA and VC losses at Tet vary between 35,000 and 50,000 but they were largely concentrated amongst the VC. So for Hanoi Tet removed the possibility of the emergence of a potential rival that could challenge its own primacy. So severe was the political eclipse of the VC as a result of Tet that it never really recovered and even in 1982 not one member of the 132-strong Central Committee came from the South. Thirdly, the Americans lost politically.

In every military sense Tet represented a massive American-ARVN success but the revelation of the enemy's capacity to mount a nationwide offensive at a time when light was supposedly at the end of the tunnel came as a traumatic experience to the American public. The television pictures of a VC squad fighting its way into the compound of the US Embassy in Saigon on 31 January raised natural question marks against Westmoreland's claims that the war was being won: if the communists could challenge the Americans in central Saigon there seemed little credibility to the claims to be winning the war up-country. Without doubt the television and press coverage of Tet was grotesquely misleading, but the American political and military leadership had only itself to blame for the inevitable reaction within America to Tet. There was a major crisis of confidence in the administration that in turn opened up various divisions within the government. No one realized it at the time, but the Tet offensive was to be the first milestone in a year that had a 'long hot summer'.

Above: A US Marine carries a wounded Vietnamese woman during the battle for Hué. Below: ARVN troops flush out Viet Cong snipers in An Quang. Below right: A North Vietnamese soldier on guard at an outpost in Hué.

Special Forces in Vietnam

American Special Forces – an all-volunteer elite, trained for unconventional warfare and usually known as the 'Green Berets' – played a unique part in the Vietnam War between 1961 and 1970. They were the only elements of the US Army devoted to the task of persuading ethnic minorities in remote areas to stand firm against VC infiltration, and the only troops actually to take on VC guerrillas using similar tactics.

Special Force operations began in late 1961 in the Montagnard village of Buon Enoa, east of Ban Me Thuot in the Central Highlands. The Montagnards, a minority ethnic group actively discriminated against by the South Vietnamese, were proving susceptible to VC subversion and the Special Force aim was to reverse this trend by offering military and civic assistance in exchange for support. The experiment worked: as local tribesmen volunteered to form a village militia, trained and led by US and ARVN Special Forces, a programme of medical, educational and agricultural aid was initiated. VC infiltration declined dramatically as the tribesmen now felt they had something worth defending, and the idea – known officially as the Civilian Irregular Defence Group (CIDG) programme – quickly spread. By 1963 the area around Ban Me Thuot could be declared 'secure' and, as similar schemes were extended to other remote areas and different ethnic minorities, Special Force commitment increased. At this stage US personnel were still theoretically 'advisers' but as American Main Force deployment to Vietnam began in 1965 the CIDG programme came under MACV control through the 5th Special Force Group (Airborne) at Nha Trang.

Above: Montagnard militia in the highlands on the Cambodian border.

It did not take long to relise that CIDG units had more than self-defence to offer, for their local knowledge and support, exploited by Special Force expertise, made them ideal 'counter-guerrilla' groups. As a result, between 1965 and 1968 the Special Forces moved onto the offensive. Camps were established, under Special Force command, in border areas to monitor and interdict VC infiltration; long-range patrols, led by Special Force officers and NCOs, were inserted deep into enemy-held areas to gather invaluable intelligence; and special mobile strike forces, drawn from CIDG units, were created to attack VC or NVA bases, often in conjunction with US or ARVN Main Force divisions. Combat was often severe – twelve Special Force members were to win the Congressional Medal of Honor in such operations – but the results were impressive. Key border areas were cleared and VC infiltration was significantly affected. Meanwhile, of course, the CIDG scheme at village level continued.

Unfortunately many of these gains were lost through Vietnamisation after 1968. The South Vietnamese continued to distrust ethnic minorities, reducing the scale of the important civic assistance programme and, in the end, insisting that the CIDG and mobile strike units be absorbed into the ARVN as ordinary conventional formations. When the 5th Special Force Group left Vietnam in December 1970, they took all the advantages with them.

J. L. PIMLOTT

Below: Troops of the CIDG prepare to engage a NVA unit around Ben Het.

Below: US counter-insurgency troops pause for a drink in the Vietnamese jungle.

4. The Political Dimension

The American public saw the full horror of the war in Vietnam daily on their television screens. As the draft bit deeper, opposition to what the US government was doing in Vietnam grew stronger, until the whole nation seemed to have split over it. The war became the most important issue in US politics. When Richard Nixon was elected president in 1968 he saw his policy as reducing American involvement, but this did not necessarily mean withdrawal of all forces. It meant 'Vietnamisation' of the ground war certainly; but Nixon was prepared to make full use of the massive airpower at his disposal – even if this meant the cynical and unauthorised bombing of Laos and Cambodia.

President Thieu of South Vietnam and President Nixon shake hands in agreement over US troop withdrawls. Behind the smile Thieu felt betrayed by what he considered to be American abandonment of South Vietnam.

The full impact of the Tet Offensive was felt in the American presidential elections of 1968. Had the nightly television news programmes not already done much to undermine official credibility, the spectacle of a Viet Cong suicide squad breaking into the supposedly impregnable US Embassy in Saigon caused a public scepticism about the Johnson administration's account of the progress of the war in a way no other event had occasioned; for Richard Nixon campaigning in the New Hampshire Republican primary 'the Vietnam war was the dominant issue – as it was throughout the campaign'. It was, moreover, an issue on which he could not lose; no one would know whether Nixon could really end the war until he was allowed to try and a regular part of his campaign speech was the promise 'New leadership will end the war and win the peace in the Pacific.' But how? Here Nixon could – smugly – act the statesman:

> As a candidate it would have been foolhardy, and as a prospective President, improper, for me to outline specific plans in detail. I did not have the full range of information or the intelligence resources available to Johnson. And even if I had been able to formulate specific 'plans', it would have been absurd to make them public. In the field of diplomacy, premature disclosure can often doom even the best-laid plans.

And the cynic might have added, the best-laid election!

Yet in a way it was logical to turn to a Republican. Johnson, in reaction to public outcry over Tet which portended electoral defeat, decided to step down; with the entry of Robert Kennedy into the race, the peace party was split in half; after his assassination, George McGovern briefly picked up his mantle thus sustaining the division. George Wallace as a third-party candidate would most likely hurt the Democrats the more; Hubert Humphrey would receive the Democratic nomination at the cost of a political indebtedness that would well-nigh cripple him. And what did he have to offer? The administration too had learned from Tet. Either there would have to be yet more escalation, mobilizing reserves, increasing taxes and generally putting the

Left: Newly elected, President Nixon discusses the military situation with General Creighton W. Abrams (next to Nixon), who took over command of US armed forces in Vietnam in 1968. Right: Vice-President Hubert Humphrey arrives in Chicago for the Democratic Convention of 1968.

country economically on a semi-war footing (incredibly, General Westmoreland asked for another 200,000 troops and then no guarantee of victory), or at long last diplomacy must substitute for force. On 1 March, Clark Clifford officially took up his post as successor to Secretary of Defense McNamara, who, increasingly disillusioned, had left for the World Bank. Was his departure there a form of atonement some wondered? In any case, the transition signified the implementation of a long-advocated policy review.

The search for peace

For Humphrey, therefore, though the review meant the president's abdication and hence opened his own path to the nomination, it also implied a repudiation of three years' policy. This was too much for Johnson. Though he would halt the bombing except on troops and supplies in the area north of the Demilitarized Zone, thus sparing 90 per cent of North Vietnam's population and most of its territory; send only 13,500 men during the next five months and welcome President Thieu's mobilization of 135,000 additional South Vietnamese towards a total military strength of 800,000 men as soon as possible, an incipient 'Vietnamization' of the war as later practised by Nixon; the peace he sought was still related to the fact that 'the heart of our involvement in South Vietnam under three different Presidents, three separate Administrations, has always been America's own security'. It was an awkward legacy for his embattled heir-apparent.

Not surprisingly the search for peace moved slowly. While Hanoi accepted Johnson's offer of talks, it had other concerns than American security. Almost the entire election campaign of 1968 passed while the two sides circled warily around each other. For several weeks, the actual site of the talks was debated; when finally in May, they got underway in Paris, deadlock resulted. The North Vietnamese wanted a complete bombing halt as a pledge of sincerity; the Americans insisted on the need to protect American troops; Hanoi would have to de-escalate as well. Not until three weeks before election day was there a breakthrough. The Americans would stop the bombing

Left: Senator Eugene McCarthy is welcomed by supporters at the Chicago Democratic Convention. Below: Vietnamese suspects are led away for questioning by US troops in the Mekong Delta.
Opposite: A Vietnamese peasant is subjected to interrogation by a member of the 1st Cavalry Division, following a search and destroy operation. American forces were never able to develop a sympathetic relationship with the South Vietnamese despite their stated aim of winning the 'hearts and minds' of the people.

in its entirety, if the North Vietnamese would guarantee the integrity of the Demilitarized Zone and not increase its aid to the Viet Cong, allow American reconnaissance flights and cease shelling South Vietnamese cities; representatives of both Saigon and the National Liberation Front (the political wing of the Viet Cong) might participate in the talks.

These developments meant that for the first time, there was the possibility that Humphrey could really be the peace candidate. In politics, as in life, nothing succeeds like success. Whereas Nixon could later claim, 'The beauty of our contest this year was that we won the nomination in a way designed to win the election,' Humphrey had been saddled with the violence of Chicago. He had emerged from the Convention there as a candidate apparently deeply flawed, Johnson's heir, seemingly obligated to machine politics of the crudest kind; any *rapprochement* with the doves, especially such fastidious ones as the McCarthy supporters, seemed well-nigh impossible. All the campaign he struggled against their slogan 'Dump the Hump'; he could neither make policy nor disown it.

The bombing stops

Nixon, in contrast, stuck to his declared position. While negotiations were going on he would not speak out; this was patriotic or politically astute depending on preference; moreover if he were to be the next president, he would be a free agent. If the war was now at long last coming to a slow but certain end, there was an argument for Nixon, whose hands were clean, in being entrusted with the responsibilities its termination would entail; a fresh start had a certain logic. To the Saigon government, the choice of Nixon also had its logic for another reason; at the very least they could do no worse with him than with Humphrey; here logic was to be bizarrely reinforced with persuasion on the eve of the election.

For Humphrey could only be made to look different and better than Nixon on the war, by the actions of Johnson; at last on Thursday, 31 October, five days before the election, the president went on television to announce that he had ordered

Above: US troops question a Viet Cong suspect. Right: A father holds the body of his son, killed as ARVN forces pursued Viet Cong guerrillas into a village near the Cambodian border. Below: Henry Kissinger – winner of the Nobel Peace Prize and one of the architects of the invasion of Cambodia.

all the bombing to cease and that formal peace talks would begin in Paris the day after the election. Had the administration strategy, at this late hour, finally reaped its reward? To Humphrey, rapidly gaining in the polls on a Nixon whose attraction had always largely been negative, it could be the decisive factor. Less than 24 hours later, his hopes were dashed; Thieu declined to participate in talks, fearing the presence of the National Liberation Front would increase its prestige: in the words of the South Vietnamese National Assembly, it was the 'betrayal of an ally'. What sort of peace then was being offered, or was it simply a Johnson dodge to help Humphrey? Only later was it generally learned that Anna Chennault, Chinese-born widow of General Claire Chennault, co-chairman of several Nixon supporters' committees, had taken it on herself to contact Saigon and offer them a 'better deal' if they refused to cooperate. Nixon privately denied all knowledge of the incident; Humphrey believed him and would not use it against him. This honourable gesture was enough to lose him the presidency.

There was, Richard Nixon had said way back in March, 'no magic formula, no gimmick. If I had a gimmick I would tell Lyndon Johnson.' Yet he had at least inherited peace talks and what was later expressly termed Vietnamization; within six months of his inauguration he would be able to formulate the Nixon doctrine which implied that elsewhere in Asia, America would avoid any more Vietnams. That lesson was palpable. On his first morning in the White House, while shaving Nixon glanced in the hidden wall-safe, noting a thin folder containing the daily Vietnam Situation Report from Johnson's last day in office. During the week ending 18 January 1969, 185 Americans had been killed, 1237 wounded. From 1 January 1968 to 18 January 1969, 14,958 men had been killed and 95,798 wounded. Sixteen years previously, Vice-President Nixon had joined Eisenhower in Washington, elected on a pledge to bring peace to Korea; sensibly and speedily Eisenhower had kept his promise. Now surely his task was to see that Johnson's war did not become Nixon's war. It was generally reckoned he had a six-month period of grace.

Kissinger's role

To a German-Jewish immigrant with memories of Nazi persecution for whom 'America acquired a wondrous quality' the issue was not so simple. 'It seemed to me important', wrote Henry Kissinger later, 'for America not to be humiliated, not to be shattered, but to leave Vietnam in a manner that even the protesters might later see as reflecting an American choice made with dignity and self-respect.'

Thus the two alternatives were formulated; withdrawal now or 'peace with honour' somewhat later. Kissinger had mentioned the protesters; it is they who had made the war issue their own and become almost symbolic of the period. The campus teach-ins, the marches, the occupation of university administration buildings, flushed out by police and tear-gas, all bespoke an opposition movement not just to the war but to much of the assumptions of the society that waged it; an H. R. Halderman would have a crew-cut, his son would wear his hair shoulder-length. One vignette of the year 1968 when America seemed to be tearing itself apart was beautifully captured by Norman Mailer at Chicago during the Democratic Convention; 3000 youths at an 'anti-birthday party' for 60-year-old Lyndon Johnson, with a song called 'Master of Hate' dedicated to him, and the audience chanting their opposition: 'No no, we won't go.'

Candidate of the silent majority

Yet Nixon owed nothing to these people; his strategy had been explicitly based on reaching out for the so-called 'Silent Majority'; were those who captured the political headlines, who seemed to have dictated the politics of the previous administration so representative? Most Americans, the Nixon campaign advisers had noted, were un-black, un-poor and un-young; to John Mitchell, for example, Nixon had a very definite constituency, and re-election in 1972 depended on satisfying and hopefully augmenting it (in this respect the attempted assassination of George Wallace in May 1972 and his withdrawal from the election was undoubtedly for Nixon a considerable political bonus); why bother about those who would never vote for him anyhow? In the moment of victory, Nixon might remember the placard seen in Desler, Ohio, in his very own middle-America, 'Bring Us Together' and aver that it 'will be the great objective of this administration at the outset, to bring the American people together', but to a man who

Above: After Tet the Americans adopted a new strategy aimed at increasing the role of the ARVN in the protection of South Vietnam and reducing the commitment of US ground forces. Below: A US Marine sets fire to a Vietnamese hut in the course of an operation against the Viet Cong.

thought that the practical effect of the demonstrators' activity 'was to give encouragement to the enemy and prolong the war', little real reconciliation was likely. Thus Nixon stated: 'To all those who would be tempted by weakness, let us leave no doubt that we will be as strong as we need to be for as long as we need to be.' Already he was sounding like Lyndon Johnson.

Sounding, however, but not necessarily acting like him. For at one level statistics tell their own story. In 1968 there were 543,000 American military forces in South Vietnam, in 1969, 475,000; in 1970 the figure had slipped to 335,000 and this was more than halved to 158,000 in 1971. On 1 September 1972 just as the presidential campaign for that year was formally starting there were but 39,000. Whereas in 1968 and early 1969 it was not uncommon for 300 Americans to be killed in a week, by the summer of 1972 it averaged perhaps three or four. And yet, and here the ambiguity of the Nixon policy is made manifest, one-third of all American deaths were to take place during Nixon's presidency.

Nixon's balancing act

For the corollary of this withdrawal required successful Vietnamization, a concept easier to formulate in the abstract; required too that the peace talks should not be allowed to stall while Hanoi waited for the balance to shift to its advantage. Nixon had to make good his intentions not to retreat ignominiously; yet any apparent bellicosity ran the risk of re-activating the anti-war elements and weakening his stance politically abroad. Hence the early decision to implement covert bombing of Viet Cong sanctuaries inside Cambodia; militarily it was hoped to reap the benefits of aggression without paying the concomitant political price. The troop withdrawals would be an indication to Hanoi of a genuine desire to seek diplomatic settlement, but not from any position of weakness; at the same time, they might help calm domestic public opinion as evidence of a real intention to wind down the war. It was a balancing act requiring considerable skill, rendered all the more difficult by the sulky stubbornness of the Saigon government and the Delphic incalculability of Hanoi.

Nixon later admitted that he 'was not personally attached to Thieu' but saw him as stronger than any likely successor; the commitment to Thieu was 'a commitment to stability'; not until the communists were prepared to cease trying to discard him, after three and a half years, in the autumn of 1972, could serious negotiations begin. Thus if Thieu was not to be abandoned he had to be supported; at the same time Hanoi had to understand that it would have to negotiate with a Nixon who meant business; he, not the Senate doves or the campus protesters would determine the timing and conditions of American withdrawal. Kissinger was soon negotiating privately with North Vietnamese representatives and in the autumn of 1969, as the anniversary of the bombing halt was approaching, Nixon faced one of his severest tests. In the face of renewed domestic protest as the university classes reopened for the fall semester, culminating in a Vietnam Moratorium demonstration in Washington on 15 October that attracted a quarter of a million people and which it was planned to repeat in different cities on the 15th of every month thereafter until the war was over, Nixon determined to secure his political base. His appeal was to 'the great silent majority'. Having pledged during the election to end the war in a way that could win the peace, he sought in a television address to undercut the influence of the protesters, 'for the more divided we are at home, the less likely the enemy is to negotiate at Paris.'

The speech was an unexpected success in rallying support for the president; his poll rating rose to a new high of 68 per cent; clearly, therefore, delayed withdrawal was a viable political option; as 1969 came to an end, still the war would go on. Now it was Nixon's war; reduced certainly, perhaps holding the prospects of a peace, but war nonetheless. And in war there is the stark alternative: to kill or be killed.

Death at Kent State

Herein lay the Alice-in-Wonderland logic of the April 1970 joint American and

Left: A hut wall is smashed by US troops on a search and destroy mission. Above: The opposition to Vietnam grew steadily in the sixties. Here, students confront police in a demonstration organized in Washington D.C. in October 1967.

Above: A protester offers a symbol of peace to an unyielding military policeman at an anti-war rally in 1967. Left: National Guardsmen are kitted out in full riot gear at Kent State University in 1970. In the clashes that occurred between students and Guardsmen on the campus, four students were left dead.

Left: Bob Hope and Connie Stevens entertain US troops in Vietnam. The US Army went to great pains to ensure that its soldiers had every comfort when out of the battle-zone. Below: One of the most telling images of the war – Vietnamese children flee the horror of a napalm strike. Opposite: A US Air Force F-100 fires a salvo of rockets at a jungle target in South Vietnam.

South Vietnamese incursions into Cambodia and the February 1971 American-supported South Vietnamese offensive into Laos; to narrow the war it was first necessary to widen it. And so, too, the demonstrations would go on. In May 1970 four students at Kent State University in Ohio protesting at the Cambodian operation would be shot on campus by National Guardsmen; all over the country universities and colleges would close; 100,000 students would gather in Washington, and Nixon in a pre-dawn walk to the Lincoln Memorial would endeavour to talk to them if not with them. Accounts differ of the conversation's effectiveness; publicly at least the myth grew that the generation gap had been too large to overcome. Yet the voice of youth can be a confused one and the activists are not necessarily typical. The same year a federal Voting Rights Act introduced a new, nationwide voting age of 18, but in 1972, of the eligible first voters (those aged 18–24) only 47 per cent actually bothered to vote.

Other protests were potentially more dangerous. If the war was unpopular at home with those who might have to take part in it, those already involved had not necessarily undergone a change of heart; even the troops were infected by the sickness. Draftees, who had no wish to be in Vietnam, soon collapsed into indiscipline, drug abuse, even mutiny as a form of escapism or resistance; alternatively, and sometimes simultaneously, there was a wanton callousness, even cruelty, of which the massacres at My Lai and Son My in March 1969 were but the most publicized examples. In 1972 there appeared an anthology of Vietnam veterans' poetry, ironically entitled *Winning the Hearts and Minds;* Larry Rottman's 'SOP' (Standard Operating Procedure) gives the flavour:

To build a 'gook stretcher', all you need is:
Two helicopters
Two long, strong ropes
And one elastic gook.

It was the inevitable concomitant of a strategy that talked of 'taking out' and 'body counts'.

Problems with Congress

Congress, too, was becoming nauseated. Controlled by the Democrats, they took steps to circumscribe the president's power. On 24 June 1970 the Senate voted by a large majority to repeal the Tonkin Gulf Resolution; on the day of the departure of US troops from Cambodia, 30 June, it passed the Cooper-Church amendment prohibiting their further use there (Nixon grumbled that it was 'the first restrictive vote ever cast on a president in wartime'); later Republican Mark Hatfield, a possible Vice-President in 1968, and Democrat George McGovern sponsored one to remove all troops by 30 June 1971.

The administration was being attacked on all fronts and a president who had just squeaked in in 1968 sensed the dangers; though he had stated on television at the time of the Cambodian operation that he accepted the risk that it would make him a one-term president, naturally enough his eyes were on 1972. Worse still there seemed to be enemies

inside his administration, of which the leaking of the Pentagon Papers, the specially commissioned study by McNamara of the American involvement in Indochina since World War II, to the *New York Times* was the most celebrated example. The administration might have been wiser to do nothing; if anything the 47 volumes made explicit the blundering, the confusion, the miscalculation with which the previous Democratic administration had led the nation into the quagmire of the Vietnam War. To Nixon, however, their publication by the *New York Times* 'was clearly the product of the paper's anti-war policy' and he moved to seek legal restraint on further disclosures. Having further embittered his already poor relations with the press, he faced the humiliation of seeing the Supreme Court in a six-to-three opinion rule that no illegality had occurred. In the words of Justice Hugo Black, 'Only a free and unrestrained press can effectively expose deception in government . . . in my view, far from deserving condemnation, for their courageous reporting, the *New York Times,* the *Washington Post* and other newspapers should be commended for serving the purpose that the Founding Fathers saw so clearly.'

The road to Watergate

To Nixon the issue was entirely different: 'I considered what Ellsberg [who had been responsible for the leaks] had done to be despicable and contemptible – he had revealed government foreign policy secrets during wartime'; he determined to get even; meanwhile there must be no more leaks. To an administration, moreover, that saw the Vietnam War as set in the wider issues of global politics and the relations between America, Russia and China, already edging towards SALT I and involved in the most secret negotiations that were to lead to the president's historic trip to China, the prospect of further damaging revelations was unthinkable. Soon the ill-omened Plumbers' Unit was set up in the Executive Office basement; from defensive it would ineluctably turn to offensive measures to silence or circumvent the administrations' critics and enemies; Nixon was on the road to Watergate.

Perhaps these two issues, the highest and the lowest of the Nixon presidency together, help explain both his success and his downfall; for Nixon had at least been elected as a fresh start. With détente with the Soviet Union and the normali-

Above: Jane Fonda lectures captured US airmen in North Vietnam. Below: After his last mission in January 1973 an American serviceman inscribes a farewell message; a sentiment shared by more than a few US troops.

Opposite top: Even as the Americans prepared to withdraw from Vietnam the fighting continued. The remains of two Vietnamese villagers killed by the Viet Cong await identification. Opposite below: After spending four years in captivity this American G.I. leaves an American hospital following treatment for wounds sustained on his capture by North Vietnamese forces.

zation of relations with China, Nixon showed that in this field at least, he could claim not to have betrayed his trust. At this momentous level of global politics, Nixon had found an issue that dwarfed even the Vietnam war; made it, in a curious way, irrelevant; as irrelevant indeed as the campaign of George McGovern whom he faced in the autumn of 1972. Nixon pre-eminently was the peacemaker even if in April 1972 he would resume limited bombing and in May, on the eve of his visit to Moscow, announce the mining of North Vietnamese ports. It was the application of the Archimedes principle to global politics; with a big enough lever one could move the world; Nixon's lever had one end in Moscow; in the words of Kissinger it was 'a carrot and a stick'. The North Vietnamese had launched a spring offensive; now 'we would not shy away from the military measures necessary . . . whatever the embarrassment this would cause the Soviet Union, whatever the risk to our relationship with Moscow, and in the face of the predictable domestic outcry. At the same time, we would put before the Soviet leaders the carrot of substantial progress in US-Soviet relations.' Thus the Russians exerted pressure on Hanoi to make peace.

America pulls out

In May Nixon stated two conditions; the return of American prisoners and an internationally supervised ceasefire – the political and military problems in Vietnam would be separated. In late October, shortly before an election that was already a foregone conclusion, Kissinger declared 'Peace is at hand.' President Thieu, however, wanted all North Vietnamese troops out of the South before he would cooperate; there were other misunderstandings, perhaps deliberately, on the part of Hanoi. Now Nixon's 'Watergate' mentality asserted itself; the ruthlessness, the vindictiveness, the willingness to take a chance. For the last terrible time, for two weeks with but a brief break over Christmas, North Vietnam would be savagely bombed by wave after wave of B-52s. In January 1973 negotiations resumed in earnest; peace seemed finally at hand.

5. Tactics and Weapons

How can an enormous arsenal designed for large scale conventional war, be adopted to winning a small-scale struggle against shadowy guerrilla fighters? This was the problem that faced the US commanders in Vietnam, and it presented difficulties they never really solved. A whole range of electronic devicies was developed; helicopters were formed into new formations; artillery was grouped into mutually supporting firebases. But the essential problem always remained: how to fight the Viet Cong on the ground – in the forests in the swamps and in the villages.

A platoon of the elite 1st Air Cavalry Division (Airmobile) land in the battle-zone as part of Operation Oregon.

Above: A squad leader of the US Marines leads his men under fire in a search and destroy mission in South Vietnam. Below: A US M48 medium tank.

In Vietnam the Americans faced a new type of conflict: General Westmoreland and his advisers had been forced into fighting a war which was as much political as military. The American armed forces were trained to undertake mobile, offensive operations that secured decisive battlefield results through the application of massive firepower. But while this tactical doctrine held good for the kind of warfare that had been waged during World War II and in Korea, the situation in Vietnam was too complex to allow for this form of conventional warfare. The major problem facing the American soldier was that there was no mutually-agreed and well-defined battlefield; the war zone was anywhere the communist enemy wished it to be and generally they refused the Americans the luxury of set-piece battles.

Search and destroy

The general American policy was actively to seek out the enemy and then destroy him – in theory very simple but in practice a problem that taxed the ingenuity of the US armed forces to the full. The Viet Cong could cease operational activity virtually at will by simply hiding their weapons and merging in with Vietnamese villagers – over whom they already had considerable control. The larger and more heavily equipped North Vietnamese (NVA) units could retire into the sanctuary areas of Laos and Cambodia and be safe from American ground force attack. Thus, except when reacting to actual communist attacks, finding the enemy to bring him into battle was the major problem for the American forces.

American strategy in Vietnam undoubtedly lacked overall coherence: a victim of the uncertainty of the politicians. The 'neutrality' of Laos and Cambodia prevented American soldiers from hunting out communist bases, until 1970, by which time the United States was embarked on a policy of withdrawal. Similarly the Demilitarized Zone (DMZ) and North Vietnam itself was denied the American Army and although such restrictive policies did much to keep international tension at a tolerable level it made fighting the North Vietnamese forces all the more difficult. Initially American ground forces had been deployed to protect American bases in South Vietnam; a perimeter defence that

left the fight against the communists in the country to South Vietnamese forces. But the failure of the perimeter defence to prevent heavily-armed VC suicide squads from breaking through defensive lines and causing havoc in air and supply bases and, more importantly, the imminent collapse of the South Vietnamese forces (ARVN) in 1965 forced the Americans to adopt a more aggressive policy by taking the war to the enemy.

From 1965 onwards the US forces prepared to accept the brunt of the fighting, a policy decision which necessitated a massive increase in manpower, so much so that by 1966 the number of troops in Vietnam had more than quadrupled from the 1965 level of 60,000 men to 268,000. But the American army that arrived in Vietnam was not necessarily suited to what had become a vicious guerrilla war. In keeping with the American tradition of providing the fighting man with maximum support service, the number of men actually fighting the VC was relatively small when set against the total figure of US troops in Vietnam. In December 1967, just before the Tet Offensive, US strength in Vietnam amounted to 473,200 men but the actual strength of combat infantry was just under 50,000 men, organized into 90 infantry battalions. In percentage figures, combat infantry amounted to just over 10 per cent of the total; artillery and engineers 12 per cent, aviation 2 per cent and the remainder – HQ and logistics troops – some 75 per cent. And as Vietnam was essentially an infantry war General Westmoreland's repeated pleas for more men were certainly understandable, if not completely justified.

Above: Marine infantrymen in the bush. Right: The M-16 rifle – a highly effective weapon used by US troops in Vietnam, shown here with a starlight night scope (above) and a grenade launcher (below).

The night belongs to Charlie

In the VC's war of attrition its greatest tactical advantage was concealment, provided by the rough and often heavily forested terrain and by darkness – a well known phrase of US troops in Vietnam was 'the night belongs to Charlie'. At night and concealed in the jungle, the VC moved supplies and men as well as laying booby traps and setting ambushes. To deny the VC concealment the American forces brought to bear all the latest technology. On the battlefield the American infantryman was provided with the 'starlight scope', a light-intensifying device that was attached to his rifle and gave the soldier reasonable vision up to a distance of 440 yards (400 metres). More powerful and sophisticated was the Night Intensification Device, a tripod-mounted light intensifier that was able to amplify the faintest light (e.g. starlight) up to 40,000 times and could, in the right conditions, detect enemy movement up to 1300 yards (1200 metres). Besides seismic surveillance devices such as ADSID (Air-Delivered Seismic Intruder Device) – used extensively on the Ho Chi Minh Trail – various types of infra-red illumination (usually helicopter-mounted) were employed to detect enemy movement through thick jungle, while ground radar with a range of up to 11,000 yards (10,000 metres), was used for long-range detection of the movement of vehicles in open country.

Locating the enemy – whether by visual or electronic means – was only the first stage; the next was to get troops to the desired location as fast as possible. This function was supplied, above all else, by the helicopter, a machine that was

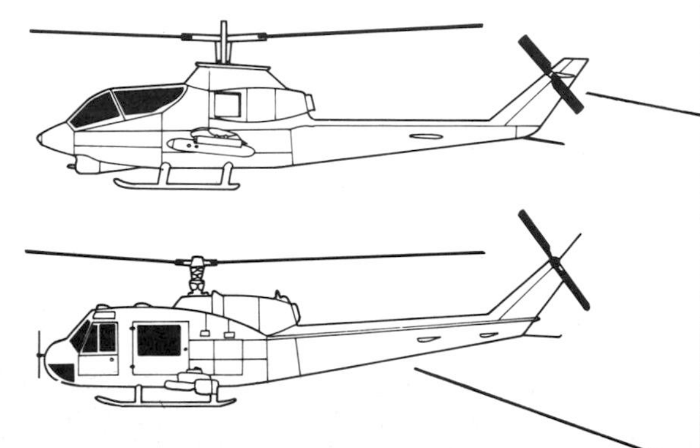

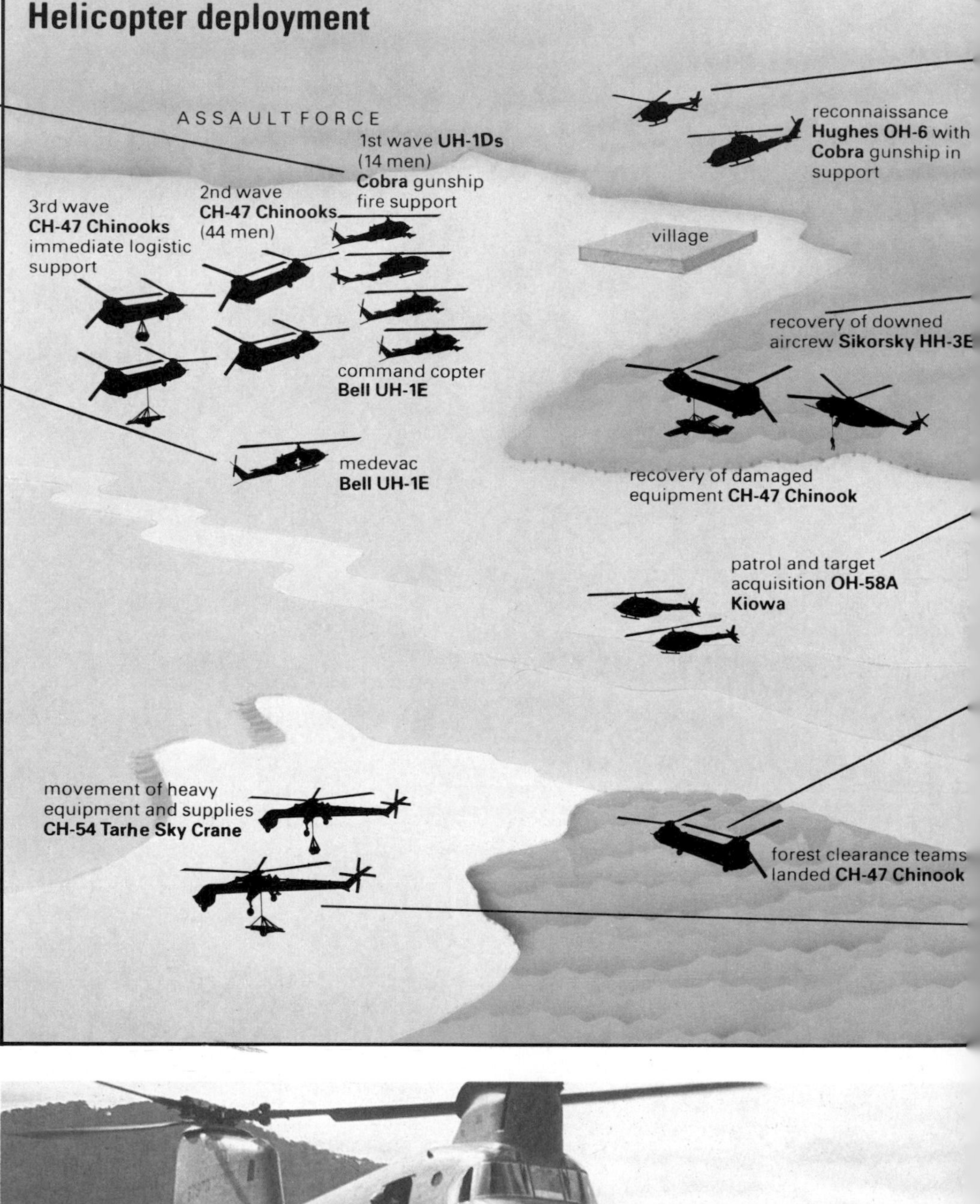

Right: The Americans used a wide variety of helicopters designed to meet the tactical problems they encountered on the battlefield. Below: The gunner of a Navy Bell UH-1 fires at a ground target in the Mekong Delta.

to play a leading part in American tactical procedure in Vietnam. Although helicopters had been used in Korea, Malaya and Algeria, it was in Vietnam that their wide-scale employment was able to transform infantry tactics.

The helicopter war

The earliest functions of the helicopter had been to facilitate communications, evacuate wounded personnel and act as an auxiliary in small unit operations. In Vietnam these functions were extended considerably to perform armed reconnaissance and fire-support duties, a role normally undertaken by the helicopter gunship – a fearsome weapon armed with a 40mm grenade launcher, a 'Gatling' mini-gun and a variety of air-to-ground rockets. Vast CH-47 Chinook and CH-54 Tahre sky-crane helicopters were used for transportation of heavy loads ranging from pieces of field artillery to damaged helicopters and light aircraft. But perhaps more important than the diversity of types of aircraft employed was the massed use of helicopters on the battlefield.

During the late sixties the Americans had some 5000 helicopters operational in Vietnam and were able to transport whole battalions of infantry at a moment's notice to selected combat zones, regard-

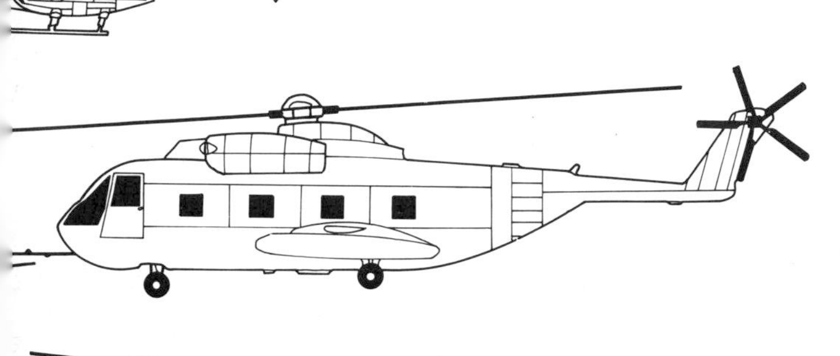

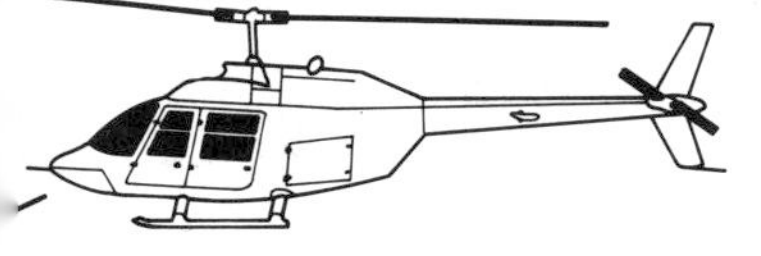

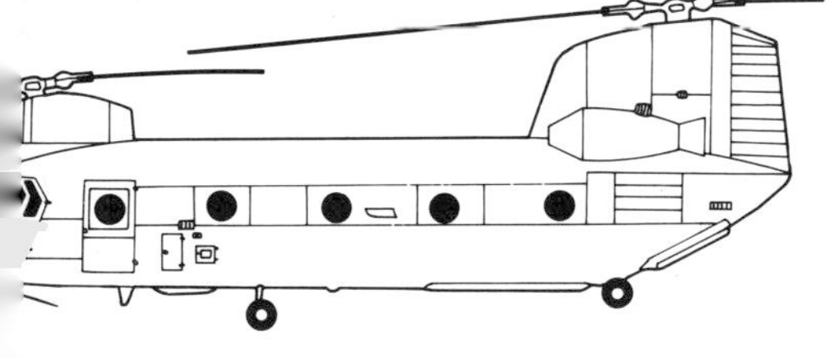

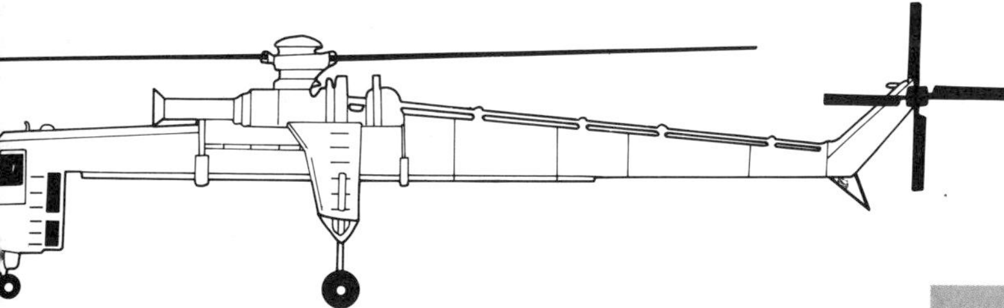

Above right: Bell UH-1Ds prepare to disembark men of the 1st Cavalry in a drive against the Viet Cong in February 1965. Above centre: A Bell UH-1D evacuates wounded Marines during an operation in July 1966. Right: A heavily-armed Bell AH-1 Huey Cobra gunship escorts a UH-1 over Quang Ngai. Left: A CH-47 Chinook supplies a 101st Airborne Division base.

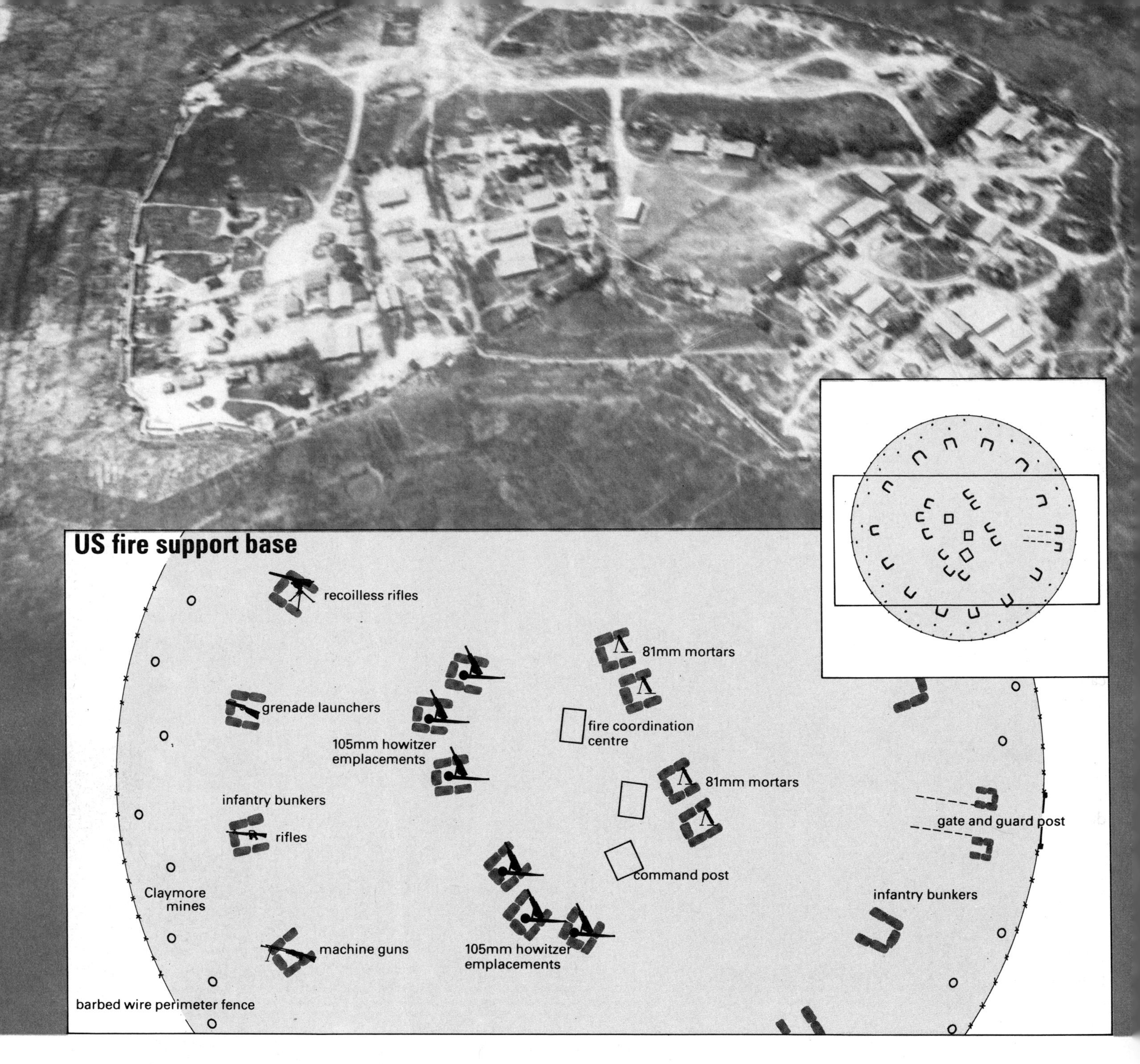

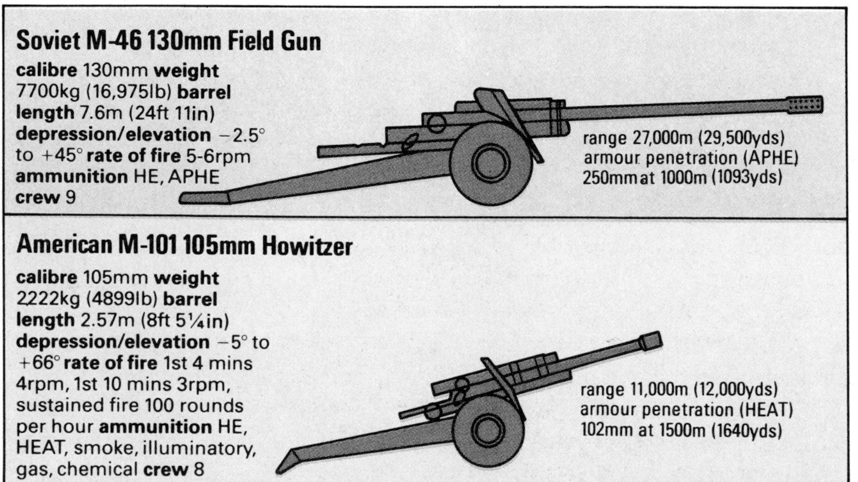

Above: US fire support bases were intended to provide a comprehensive and flexible support for the infantry in the field. Left: Although the US 105mm howitzer was a light and manoeuvrable weapon it was outranged by the Soviet-built 130mm field gun that was used by the North Vietnamese Army.

less of terrain. This air mobility was exploited to the full and allowed the anti-communist forces to transport their elite troops to shore up danger spots or to prosecute suprise attacks against enemy positions, as was the case in the invasion of Cambodia in 1970 when small pockets of NVA troops were caught in the open and slaughtered by US gunships.

The helicopter concept was taken to the extent of forming airmobile divisions – crack formations consisting of around 15,000 men with over 400 aircraft organized into three helicopter battalions, plus complete artillery, infantry, engineer, signals and logistic support. The creation of such a large and specialized formation as the airmobile division was a controversial decision but one which proved itself successful in practice, providing the American field commander with the two assets he most urgently required – firepower and mobility.

While helicopters allowed the American Army to fight its own type of war, it is arguable that in making operations fit the requirements of the helicopter, reliance on airmobile warfare worked against overall American strategy. Because airmobile units flew out to specific incidents and then returned to base, they had only a limited and usually negative contact with the local population and so did little to help the 'Hearts and Minds' strategy that was supposedly at the centre of American anti-guerrilla operations. Also, the growing dependence on the helicopter made basic operational activities hazardous when extraneous factors like bad weather prevented helicopter support.

Fire support bases

In order to gain territorial control of contested regions in a manner impossible to the helicopter, the US Army developed the Fire Support Base (FSB) system. In essence the FSB was a self-contained artillery position sited at a commanding geographic point that dominated the surrounding countryside and provided support for ground forces within artillery range. In theory, at least, the FSB system was intended to be mutually supporting so that if one base came under attack other, adjacent bases could provide supporting artillery fire; but problems of terrain and limited American resources made the mutually supportive FSB more an exception than a rule. A typical fire base might have a battery of six 105mm howitzers and four 81mm mortars as well as an infantry battalion and support services. The firebase performed useful functions in allowing the Americans a considerable degree of physical control of the countryside around the base. In addition, they provided an attractive and seemingly vulnerable target for North Vietnamese attacks which would make the communists concentrate their forces in sufficient strength to allow the US Army to locate them and bring them to battle. Once battle was joined superior American organization and firepower invariably won the day.

But if airmobile warfare was not a complete solution, neither was the FSB system. As the firebases were often sited in remote positions they were vulnerable to North Vietnamese attack and with the introduction into the NVA of the Soviet 130mm field gun – a weapon which easily outranged the US 105mm howitzer – the firebases were at a decided disadvantage, and during severe assaults had to be 'rescued' by massive tactical air assaults on communist positions and by the quick arrival of heliborne reinforcements.

Riverine warfare

The Mekong Delta is a region of marshes and swamp which made both firebases and conventional infantry patrols impracticable. The solution was the formation of the Riverine Force consisting of elements of the navy and the army working in conjunction with the ARVN to deny the enemy the use of the network

Top: The long barrel of the M-46 130mm field gun can be clearly seen in this photograph. Centre: A strongly-armoured monitor sails up a waterway in South Vietnam. Above: A vessel of a US assault group patrols an area of marshland in the Mekong Delta.

of canals and rivers of the southern provinces so closely sited to Saigon. In order to overcome the physical problems of the swamp, flotillas of fast patrol boats cruised up and down the waterways, while in more difficult conditions monitors and Patrol Air Cushion Vehicles (PACVs) were employed. The monitors were heavily-armed and heavily-armoured gun-boats capable of leading assaults against defended positions, while the PACVs worked on the hovercraft principle and were able to travel over water, marsh and land, thus allowing the Americans great operational flexibility in the Delta.

An alienated population

It was one of the great paradoxes of the Vietnam War that the American forces – well-led, well-organized and well-armed and equipped – failed to defeat the VC and the NVA. On the battlefield itself the US Army always did well, sometimes winning brilliant tactical victories against the communists, but on the strategic level American policy failed miserably. Always too reliant on expensive technological solutions to simple tactical problems and weighed down by an enormous logistical system, the American war machine proved an ungainly monster. The key to the war – as the Americans were the first to admit – lay in winning over the people to the anti-communist cause but US tactical policies in Vietnam, in effect, did just the opposite. Saturating vast areas of the countryside with massive bombardments led to many civilian casualties and an awesome refugee problem. Such tactics alienated the population and made it easy for the VC to present the American forces as yet another uncaring colonial oppressor. Had the US army gone out from their bases and developed closer ties with the South Vietnamese people and their local village organizations, and, at the same time, been prepared to outfight the communists in the jungle, the outcome of the war in Vietnam might have been different.

Falling morale

A serious problem facing American commanders was the deterioration of Army morale in the late sixties. As the draft bit deeper into American society there was a growing reluctance amongst the conscripted soldiers to go out and fight in a war that meant little or nothing to them.

A further problem acting against morale was growing drug abuse. The availability of drugs in South Vietnam – especially Saigon – gave the consumer-conscious American armed forces easy access to marijuana and hard drugs opium, morphine and heroin. Between January 1967 and December 1968 the rate of marijuana use in the Army rose by some 18-fold, and in 1970 the number of drug cases was 11,058 whereas in 1967 it had been only 1391.

The drug problem was compounded by racial tensions: many blacks claimed that the draft laws operated unfairly against them and there was increasing resentment shown by black other-ranks towards their white officers. However, the hostility felt by the conscripted soldier towards the professional officers and NCOs was a general phenomanon that crossed racial boundaries. In extreme cases this led to 'fragging': the assassination of over-zealous officers and NCOs who were considered by their men to run up too high a casualty rate; this form of assassination often being effected by a fragmentation grenade.

Whereas elite units and formations like the Special Forces and the 1st Cavalry Division (Airmobile) thrived in Vietnam, for the infantry footsloger the war was a hateful business of booby traps and sudden ambushes from an unseen enemy. Nonetheless the US armed forces, for all their problems – not the least of them being a combat-hardened and resolute enemy – fought well. American units never broke and ran, even in the most extreme cases brought about by heavy battlefield casualties, but always struggled through – even if they had little enthusiasm for the war.

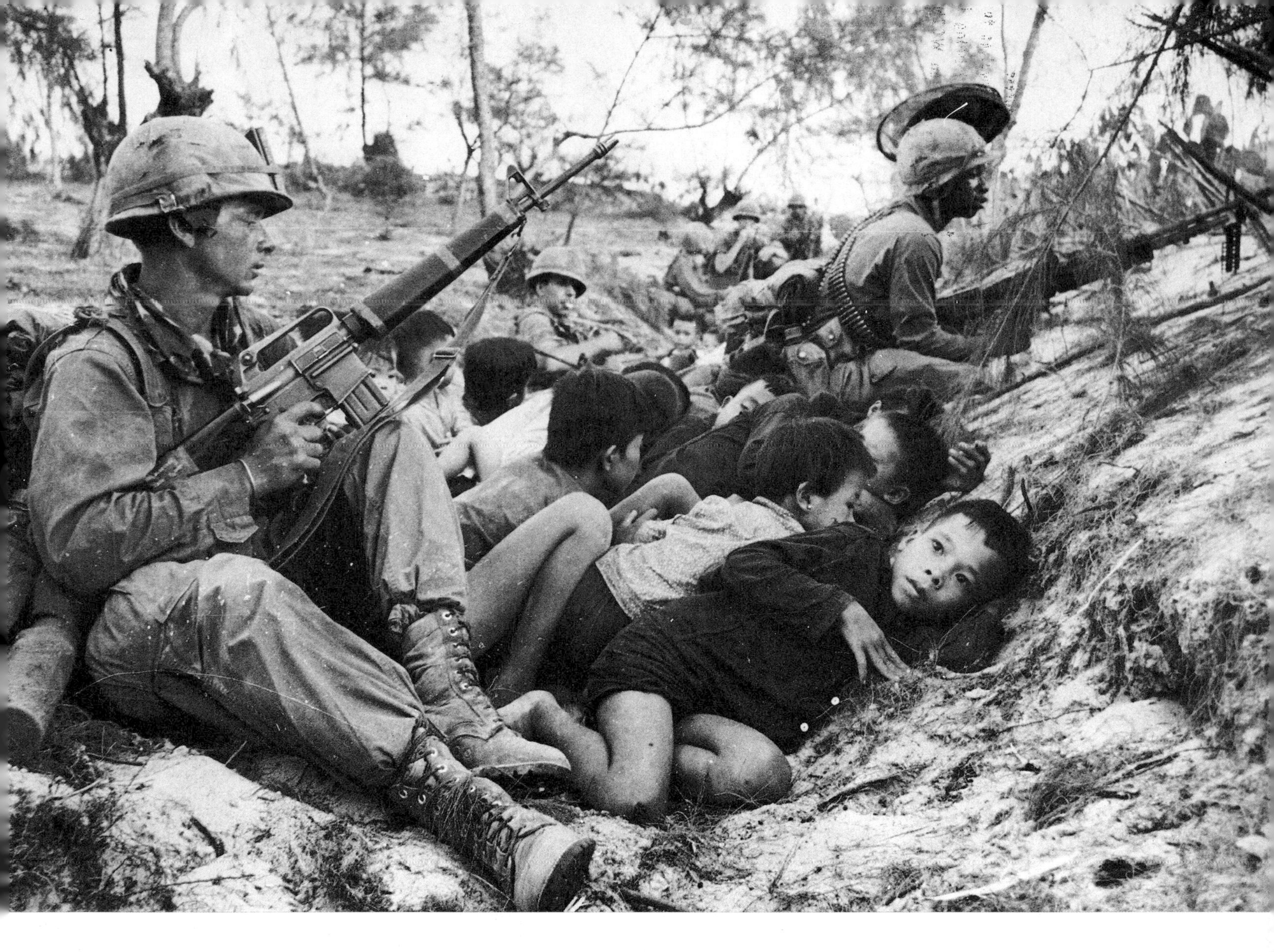

Opposite above: One of the most versatile craft was the PACV which saw extensive use in US riverine operations. Opposite below: Elite troops of the US Navy SEALS (Sea, Air, Land) hit the shore in an operation in the Rung Sat special zone. Above: Men of the 1st Cavalry and South Vietnamese children come under sniper fire south of Da Nang. Right: A Viet Cong tunnel system is uncovered by troops of the 7th Marines; dead Viet Cong litter the entrance.

6. Laos and Cambodia

Laos and Cambodia, Vietnam's western neighbours, had political and military histories of their own, but they were forced to respond to the growing intensity of the war in Vietnam. The Vietnamese communists used them as a supply route and a safe refuge; in return the Americans and South Vietnamese bombed and raided them. And both sides in the Vietnam War tried to restructure the polities of these countries in their own image. Neutralist elements in Vientiane and Phnom Penh struggled in vain to prevent their nations from succumbing to the whirlwind of the war, and to avert the tragedy that eventually became inevitable.

Troops of the Khmer Rouge prepare a punji-stick booby-trap in the forests of Cambodia. Although well-armed with Type-56 assault rifles and RPG-7 rocket launchers the Khmer Rouge still made use of primitive booby-traps such as the one shown here.

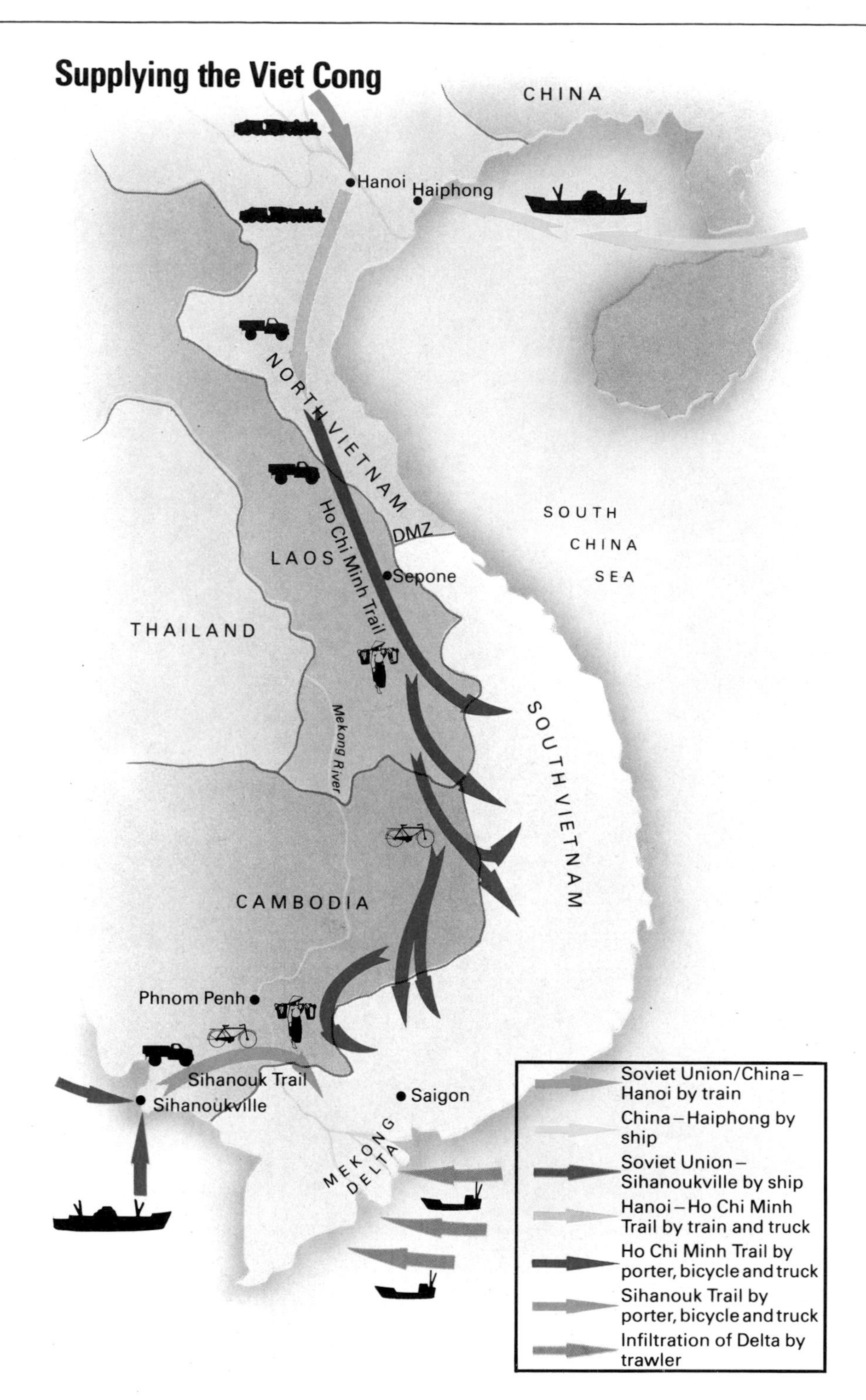

One of the great tragedies of the Vietnam War was the unwanted involvement of Laos and Cambodia in the conflict. Such an involvement was inevitable, however, both for geographical and historical reasons. The physical shape of Vietnam, and the division of North from South on the narrow corridor of land on the 17th parallel, made it impossible for the North Vietnamese to wage a guerrilla war in the South without making extensive use of the 'sanctuary' and supply-route facilities that were available in Laos and Cambodia. South Vietnam and America, for their part, were unwilling to let the Vietnamese communists have free range in Laos and Cambodia and so, inexorably, the war in Vietnam spilled over into the two adjacent countries.

As Laos, Cambodia and Vietnam had been part of French Indochina, administrative and linguistic ties remained, and North Vietnam had a strong interest in forming an 'Indochinese Union', with North Vietnam, of course, as the dominant partner – despite occasional denials of that intention. The Laotians and Cambodians understandably failed to share their aggressive neighbour's enthusiasm for such a union; there had been a long history of conflict between the racially dissimilar Vietnamese and the Lao and Khmer (Cambodian) peoples. In many respects the history of Laos and Cambodia, following the French withdrawal in 1954, was the story of their attempt – ultimately unsuccessful – to preserve their neutrality and independence against foreign aggressors.

Laotian nationalism

The ease with which the Japanese ousted the imperial powers from their Asian colonies during World War II was a great encouragement to the formation of indigenous nationalist parties determined to overthrow the yoke of colonial oppression. In Laos, opposition to the resumption of French rule was centred around the nationalist Lao Issarah (Free Laotian Party) which was led by two royal half-brothers, Prince Souvanna Phouma and Prince Souphanouvong. Talented leaders with the twin advantages of an acute political sense and the respect of the peasantry, they were to play leading roles in Laotian politics over the next 30 years – though in very different ways.

In 1949 the French granted Laos a limited degree of independence, a decision which, however, split Lao Issarah. Prince

Opposite page: The vulnerability of South Vietnam to communist infiltration is shown in this map: not merely content to use Laos and Cambodia as supply routes the Vietnamese communists exploited the marshy regions of the Mekong Delta as a way of supporting their men in the South. Above: North Vietnamese troops move forward in a massed attack during the fighting in Laos. Right: Troops of the Pathet Lao undergo a roll-call. Anti-aircraft machine guns of Soviet origin are visible in the foreground. Below: Female soldiers of the People's Militia on patrol in the northern Laotian province of Nam Tha. Bordering on China, Nam Tha was always threatened by periodic Chinese incursions.

Souvanna Phouma accepted the French plan while Prince Souphanouvong set up the Pathet Lao (Land of the Lao), backed by the Viet Minh. The Pathet Lao saw themselves as carrying on the tradition of resistance of the Lao Issarah but in fact they were very much a puppet of the North Vietnamese communists.

At the 1954 Geneva Conference, which followed the French defeat at Dien Bien Phu, the Viet Minh agreed to withdraw from Laos (an undertaking they soon broke) while the Pathet Lao were withdrawn to the two northernmost provinces bordering China, Phong Saly and Sam Neua. This was in effect a de facto partition of the country, as the Pathet Lao took control of these provinces while the Royal Government ruled over the remainder.

Despite intermittent guerrilla activity, attempts were made to integrate the Pathet Lao into the Kingdom of Laos, with some, though limited, success. Under the name of Neo Lao Hati Sat (Patriotic Front of Lao) the Pathet Lao entered into Laotian parliamentary politics and did well in the 1958 elections.

Royalists, communists and neutrals

By the end of the fifties three factions had emerged on the Laotian political scene: the Pathet Lao, the American-backed Royal Government and a loose collection of neutralists who from time to time would side with either of the other two factions. Increasingly, however, there was a growing polarization in Laos between right and left which burst into open conflict when in January 1960 the right-wing and pro-American General Phoumi Nosavan seized control of the government. Prince Souphanouvong was arrested but escaped and fled to North Vietnam.

In reply to the right-wing coup, neutralist factions under paratroop commander Kong Le captured Vientiane and urged the return to a neutralist government under the leadership of Souvanna Phouma. However, American aid was given to the right-wing faction who recaptured Vientiane in December 1960 and set up a government under the control of Prince Boun Oum. The Pathet Lao, who held on to the northern and eastern areas of the country, were given increasing amounts of aid from North Vietnam and the Soviet Union, and were joined in an uneasy alliance by the remainder of Kong Le's neutralist forces.

Worried by the violent turn of events in Laos, a 14-nation conference was convened in Geneva to attempt to resolve the crisis and a ceasefire was agreed upon by the warring factions. After much wrangling a coalition government was set up in June 1962 with Souvanna Phouma as prime minister, a position he was to occupy until 1975 despite a number of attempted right-wing coups, aimed at pushing Laos into a pro-American alliance.

American involvement

During the sixties American involvement in Laos increased considerably as large supplies of money and arms were provided for the Royal Laotian Government in their struggle against the Pathet Lao and the North Vietnamese. Much of this aid came via the CIA who organized two airlines as fronts for their activities. Unfortunately the CIA operations attracted more than their usual share of adventure-seekers and mercenaries, who carried out their cloak-and-dagger duties with great technical skill but with little regard for overall American policy. Different elements in American government found themselves working at cross purposes and at times even working against each other. In 1960, for example, the CIA and the

US Air Force C-123s spray defoliants over a valley in 1967.

A Huey Cobra gunship of the US Marine Corps.

The result of an American bombing mission.

Defense Department supported General Phoumi Nosavan's coup in disregard of the State Department who favoured Prince Souvanna Phouma.

More damaging still was the way American aid disrupted the already fragile Laotian political and economic system. Instead of strengthening the social fabric of the country the aid remained in the hands of the government and exacerbated the rift between the poverty-stricken countryside and the middle-class populations in the towns. Thus, while the position of the rural peasantry declined steadily through the deprivations of war, urban centres such as Vientiane were flooded with American money and became consumer-goods boom towns – a state of affairs that played directly into the hands of Pathet Lao propaganda.

As the government lost touch with its people through its reliance on foreign support, so did the 70,000-strong Royal Laotian Army, a force that never attempted to go out into the country to tackle the guerrilla forces of the Pathet Lao head-on, confining itself, instead, to seasonally organized, conventionally-mounted campaigns in the Plain of Jars. Indeed, much of the real fighting was undertaken by Meo and Kha tribesmen who were paid, armed and organized by the Americans. The Meo Army under the leadership of General Vang Pao fluctuated in size but reached a peak in 1970, when there were an estimated 40,000 tribesmen pitted against the Pathet Lao and North Vietnamese Army (NVA).

Communist advantages

The Pathet Lao numbered around 35,000 men in the early sixties and although numbers dropped during the decade, they were able to sustain a concerted guerrilla operation against the Royal Government forces. Organized along Viet Cong lines the Pathet Lao operated amongst the people and were able to gain their support. Highly disciplined, they gave practical aid to the peasantry who in return saw them not as terrorists but as benefactors.

The Pathet Lao also adroitly manipulated ethnic minorities to their advantage. While the Americans simply bought the loyalty of the Meo and Kha tribes, the Pathet Lao integrated them into their organizations, setting up the Meo Resistance League under Phay Dong, who was given ministerial status in Souphanouvong's 'government of resistance'. The Kha tribal leader Sithone Komadam was also made a minister; in this way the Pathet Lao cleverly manipulated the age-old animosity of the Kha towards the Laotians.

Although the North Vietnamese gave material support to the Pathet Lao, the large numbers of NVA troops in Laos did little actual fighting against the Royal Laotian Government. Instead, their main duties were the protection and administration of the Ho Chi Minh Trail, the importance of which increased as the war in South Vietnam developed. The Laotian government was unable (and unwilling) to take on the North Vietnamese and so it was forced to accept the existence of the Trail, leaving the Americans to deal with the problem.

Bombing the Trail

The American response was to mount a ferocious bombing campaign. During the period 1965–71, US forces dropped more than 2.2 million tons of bombs on the Ho Chi Minh Trail in Laos – more than the entire figure for US bombing in all theatres of operations during World War II. Despite the intensity of the bombing, which was extended to other parts of the country, the supply activities of the North Vietnamese continued unchecked down the Trail. In fact, the bombing of Laos was counter-productive to America and her allies, destroying vast areas of the countryside, turning the people against the Americans and creating a massive refugee problem (an estimated 700,000 by 1970 out of a population of two million) without materially affecting the capabilities of the Pathet Lao or NVA.

While the United States conducted a vigorous, though covert, campaign against the communist forces in Laos, they were reluctant to formally commit ground forces. And yet despite all the efforts of the American advisers and the USAF bombers, they had signally failed to prevent the North Vietnamese from using the Laotian panhandle to transport men and supplies down to South Vietnam.

To solve the problem, the American military favoured a ground-force invasion in southern Laos with the intention of physically severing the Ho Chi Minh Trail, and General Westmoreland had gone as far as to prepare a detailed plan of operation. The generals were overruled, however, as the American planners prepared to destroy the Trail through technology. Millions of dollars were spent in research programmes to develop extraordinarily complex and ingenious surveillance devices that would monitor troop and truck movements on the Trail and allow the airforce to destroy the Viet Cong at selected spots. Known as *Igloo White*, the surveillance programme took a variety of forms using airborne radar, infra-red and white light intensifying devices as well as the mass sowing of camouflaged Air Delivered Seismic Intruder Devices (ADSID), able to detect the vibrations from the movement of men as well as vehicles.

Despite the sophistication of *Igloo White*, it failed in its primary objective of drying up the Ho Chi Minh Trail, which expanded its operation through-

A flight of B-52 bombers unload their deadly cargo. Originally planned as an aircraft capable of delivering nuclear weapons, the B-52 was widely used in Vietnam in a tactical role, being capable of carrying a conventional bomb-load of over 30 tons.

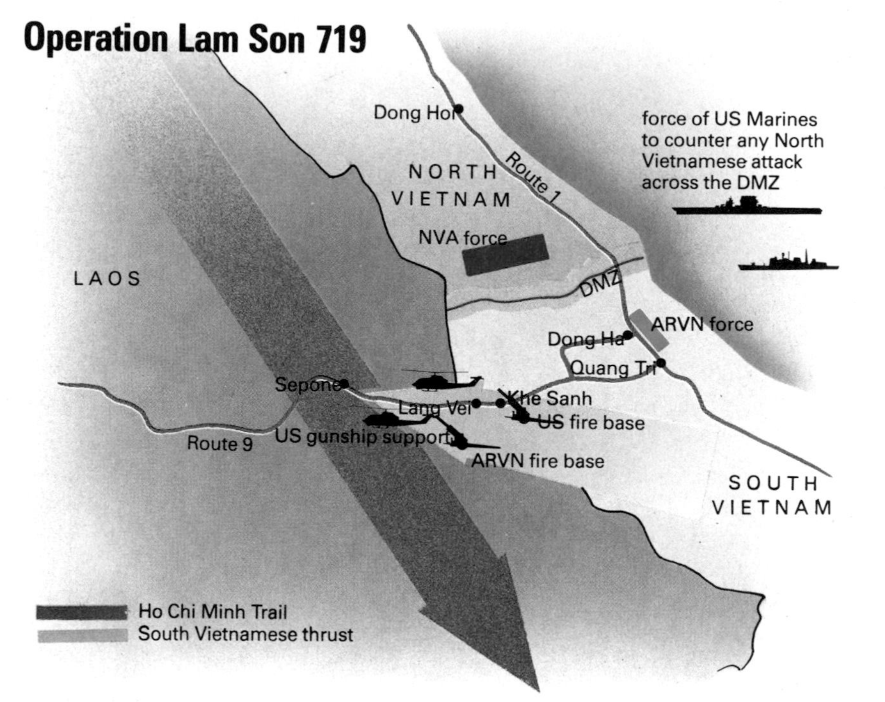

out the sixties. In 1968 alone, for example, it was estimated that from 100,000 to 150,000 VC and NVA troops had moved down the Trail.

Lam Son 719

At the close of 1970 it was decided to mount an invasion (codename *Lam Son 719*) of southern Laos, but for political reasons only South Vietnamese (ARVN) troops would actually cross the border, the Americans providing air and artillery support. In the January of 1971 forward artillery bases were set up at Lang Vei and Khe Sanh. On 8 February the main invasion force pushed over the border with the objective of capturing the small town of Sepone, 22 miles (35 km) inside Laos – a sufficient distance, it was argued, to sever the Trail. Bad weather slowed the ARVN assault, however, and by 19 February the advance had all but ground to a halt 15 miles (24 km) in from the border.

Realizing that this was more than just a diversionary raid, the North Vietnamese reacted swiftly and resistance to the ARVN stiffened. Calling upon American air support, the ARVN commander, General Lam, helicoptered two battalions of ARVN infantry to Sepone which was captured with little resistance on 6 March. But as the ARVN troops prepared to withdraw, communist forces launched a counter-attack which caught the South Vietnamese by surprise and there was an element of panic as the troops crowded into American helicopters to fly them back to Vietnam.

Despite South Vietnamese and American claims to the contrary, Operation *Lam Son 719* was an almost complete failure. The number of ARVN troops available to launch the invasion was completely inadequate – the American plan of the mid sixties had envisaged an invasion force of around 60,000 men while the ARVN had only 17,000 available. Consequently, they were unable to hold their already limited objectives and when hard-pressed by the enemy, they had to be quickly air-lifted out of the danger zones. More damning still, because the objectives were so limited they had little effect on cutting the flow of communist supplies; the North Vietnamese simply moved the Trail a few miles westward out of the combat zone. Despite South Vietnamese claims that they had severely disrupted the flow of supplies, later reconnaissance reports suggested that the flow of vehicles on the Trail had actually doubled from 1000 trucks a day to around 2000.

Opposite page: Its limited objectives compromised by insufficient forces, Lam Son *719 was doomed never to succeed. Opposite far left: The effect of saturation bombing by US B-52s. Opposite left: ARVN troops briefly occupy a road on the Ho Chi Minh Trail. Right: A 37mm anti-aircraft gun manned by troops of the Pathet Lao. At first sight an archaic form of defence against American jet aircraft, anti-aircraft guns such as this one accounted for a surprisingly high number of US aerial losses. Below: Prince Norodom Sihanouk kept Cambodia on a neutral course until his overthrow by Lon Nol in 1970.*

Bankrupt of other options, the Americans continued their mass bombing campaign of Laos.

Souphanouvong's victory

Meanwhile, the Pathet Lao mounted a major assault on the Plain of Jars in the summer of 1970 which threw the government forces back towards the old city of Luang Prabang. In the north of Laos the American-aided Meo tribesmen were on the verge of defeat as NVA troops began to flush them out of their mountain strongholds. The Laotian War was entering a new phase as the communist forces took the initiative.

In February 1973, Souvanna Phouma, realizing the desperate military position of the Royal Government, managed to negotiate a ceasefire with the Pathet Lao in the hope of securing a compromise political settlement. Fighting quickly flared up again, however, as the communists made further territorial gains in Laos. The government troops were forced back towards the western borders of the country and by the spring of 1975 even the stronghold at Vientiane was threatened by Pathet Lao troops. In June Vientiane was taken over by the communists and the war was virtually at an end. Prince Souvanna Phouma's coalition was abolished as a new communist state came into being with Prince Souphanouvong as president.

The land of the Khmer

In Cambodia, as in both Laos and Vietnam, the defeat of the Japanese in 1945 saw a new anti-colonial spirit which saw its expression in the nationalist Khmer Issarah (Free Cambodia) party – a non-communist, monarchist organization controlled by Prince Norodom Sihanouk. Under Sihanouk, Cambodia won many concessions from the French – who were preoccupied with Vietnam – and in 1955 he became premier. In 1960 he was appointed president – a position he was to hold for the next 10 years.

Sihanouk was both an autocratic and enlightened ruler, and as a confirmed neutralist he did everything in his power to keep Cambodia out of the Vietnamese conflict. No friend of communism, he ruthlessly suppressed communist and other left-wing groups. Supported by the Viet Minh, Cambodian communists mounted an insurgency campaign in the rural and eastern provinces of the country during the early fifties, though it was not until the late sixties that this campaign began to put the government in danger. The real threat to Sihanouk's rule came, in fact, from the Americans, who strongly disapproved of his neutralist policies. CIA-funded right-wing elements in Cambodia were trying to force the government away from neutrality towards a pro-American stance. The most powerful of these groups was the Khmer Seria (Free Khmers), a right-wing insurgency force that operated from Thailand. Relations between the Cambodian government and the United States were consequently poor – with Sihanouk accusing the CIA of fostering rebellion in Cambodia – and in 1965 Cambodia broke off diplomatic relations.

The bombing begins

As the momentum of the Vietnam War increased during the sixties, so too did the role of the Ho Chi Minh Trail in Cambodia. Unable to stop the Viet Cong and

Above: A soldier of the Khmer Rouge prepares to fire a Soviet built RPG-7 portable rocket launcher. Below: North Vietnamese troops, armed with captured US bazookas, march down the Ho Chi Minh Trail in Cambodia.

NVA making use of the border regions of Cambodia, Sihanouk reluctantly accepted their presence. The relationship between North Vietnam and Cambodia was always an uneasy one and Sihanouk tried unsuccessfully to limit VC and NVA activities, realizing that communist military operations emanating from Cambodia would increase the chances of full-scale American and South Vietnamese invasion.

Apart from a few covert raiding parties, the Americans had kept out of Cambodia but after 1968 they began to mount a series of massive bombing strikes against the southern and eastern provinces. Some 3630 secret B-52 raids had been conducted against Cambodia prior to March 1970, causing widespread destruction but without seriously affecting Viet Cong activities. The North Vietnamese actually expanded their operations when they began to ship in supplies from the Cambodian coast at Sihanoukville. The 'Sihanouk Trail', as it was called, was a useful supplement to the war-ravaged and much longer Ho Chi Minh Trail.

By the end of the sixties, Cambodia was at crisis point. The economic situation was steadily worsening and while Sihanouk was highly regarded by the peasantry there was growing dissatisfaction with his autocratic rule, which was used by right-wingers and communist sympathizers alike in their attempts to overthrow him.

Lon Nol seizes power

Sihanouk underestimated the dangers of the internal political situation and in the spring of 1970 he travelled to Europe to gain support and aid for Cambodia. On 13 March he flew to Moscow in an attempt to persuade the Soviet government to pressure North Vietnam to decrease its activities in Cambodia. On the 18th, right-wing elements mounted a coup and overthrew the Sihanouk government, replacing it with a pro-American, anti-communist regime under the presidency of Sihanouk's former prime minister, Lon Nol.

Sihanouk took refuge in Peking where he joined various groups active in attempting to bring down the Lon Nol government. These included the communist Khmer Rouge (whom, ironically, he had suppressed in the fifties), and because of his international reputation he became the leading spokesman for the Cambodian rebels.

Rather than restoring order the coup furthered the collapse of Cambodia as the forces of right and left intensified their struggle for control of the country. One of the first acts of the new Cambodian government was to close Sihanoukville – renamed Kompong Som – to the North Vietnamese, thereby blocking the point of entry for the Sihanouk Trail. The Cambodian Army was rapidly expanded from less than 40,000 men in Sihanouk's time to 200,000 men. There was no corresponding increase in quality, however, and the army was unable to mount major operations in the field. In many instances it merely carried out a pointless, though vicious, pogrom against the Vietnamese minority population and the many Vietnamese refugees who had fled to Cambodia when it had been a relative haven of peace. The North Vietnamese increased their own forces in Cambodia so that by March 1970, US intelligence estimated the presence of around 40,000 VC supported by 5000 NVA regulars in the country.

The American authorities were understandably worried by the increase in communist activity in Cambodia, and in 1970 the political leaders relented to pressure from the US military to mount a limited invasion of Cambodia. As part of the US policy of Vietnamization the bulk of the ground forces were to be supplied by the ARVN while the Americans concentrated on providing air and logistical support.

Parrot's Beak and Fish Hook

The invasion plan was to make a number of separate attacks on what were thought to be major Viet Cong sanctuaries, destroy them and then retire. The first major assault was launched on 29 April by ARVN troops against the Parrot's Beak, an area of Cambodia protruding

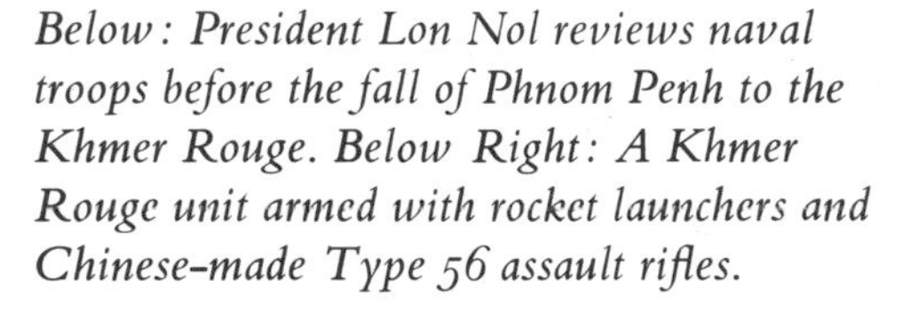

Below: President Lon Nol reviews naval troops before the fall of Phnom Penh to the Khmer Rouge. Below Right: A Khmer Rouge unit armed with rocket launchers and Chinese-made Type 56 assault rifles.

into South Vietnam. With lavish numbers of light tanks and armoured personnel carriers and with complete command of the air, the 12,000-strong ARVN force plunged quickly into Cambodia and, in a series of efficiently conducted search and sweep operations, captured tons of supplies and military equipment for only minimal casualties – the Viet Cong having retired deeper into Cambodia.

Further north a second invasion was mounted by both US and ARVN troops against Cambodian territory known as the Fish Hook. In this area it was thought that the Central Office for South Vietnam (COSVN) was stationed – the combined military and political headquarters for spearheading the war in South Vietnam. The invasion was preceded by a short but massive B-52 and artillery bombardment. Again, little resistance was met with and on 7 May a vast encampment complex known as the 'City' was discovered which contained 300 bunkers, 800 camouflaged huts and many miles of tunnels as well as a substantial arms haul which included 1.5 million rounds of small-arms ammunition. A number of other raids were conducted to the north of the Fish Hook and other Viet Cong supply bases were discovered, although without successfully engaging the enemy; the COSVN itself, however, was never found.

American withdrawal

In America there was fierce opposition to the invasion from the anti-war movement, and having seemed to have fulfilled their primary objectives US troops withdrew from Cambodia at the end of June, leaving the ARVN to conduct sporadic operations against Viet Cong units. Most ARVN units had similarly withdrawn from Cambodia by July, while the Viet Cong returned to their old sanctuary bases. Although the US/ARVN expedition had captured large supplies of arms and equipment (estimates ranged from 30 to 50 per cent of all that possessed by the Viet Cong in Cambodia) they had once again failed to destroy the communist capability to carry on the war.

One of the stated objectives of the American invasion had been to relieve the communist pressure on Lon Nol's government forces but in this the Americans were even less successful than they had been in destroying Viet Cong sanctuary bases. During 1970 the Cambodian communist forces, by then known as the Khmer Rouge, were mounting a ferocious campaign which had secured them control of most of the countryside. Although the Americans had helped finance the coup which brought Lon Nol to power, not wishing to be involved in a new war, they sent only limited supplies of military aid to the new government. Lon Nol made repeated entreaties for military assistance, but US aid consisted of a shipment of World War II vintage small arms and a few modern machine-guns, while the South Vietnamese turned over their captured communist weapons, consisting of several thousand AK47 rifles. Such aid was clearly insufficient to deal with the politically motivated Khmer Rouge.

Phnom Penh besieged

During 1971-2, the Khmer Rouge successfully won the battle for the countryside, and well armed with weapons and equipment supplied by the North Vietnamese, they began to push Lon Nol's troops back towards the Cambodian capital, Phnom Penh. The Cambodian government was in a perilous position: Lon Nol had proved to be a poor administrator and the strain of recent events had shattered his health both physically and mentally. Power was gradually being taken over by the deputy premier Sirik Matik but he too was unable to stem the communist tide.

The Khmer Rouge had originally been envisaged by the North Vietnamese as a subordinate organization along the lines of the Laotian Pathet Lao, but by the early seventies the Khmer Rouge had shaken off the controls of Hanoi and, much to the consternation of the North Vietnamese, they began to look towards China for support. Although Prince Sihanouk was nominally leader of the Cambodian rebel forces, real power was vested in Pol Pot, a shadowy figure who exercised a brutal authority over the Khmer Rouge.

By the end of 1973 only the area around

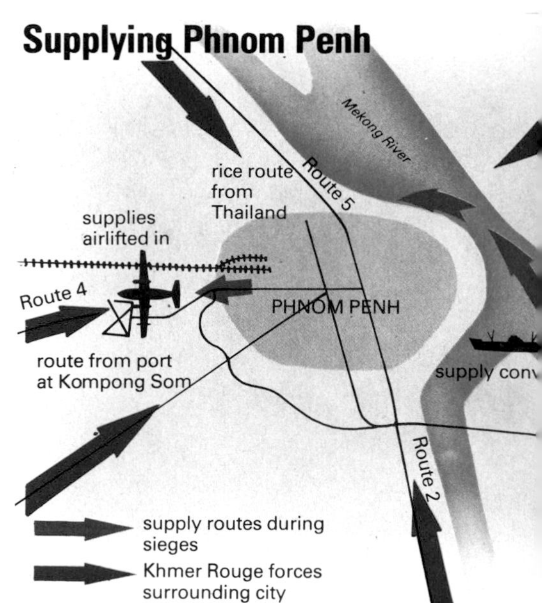

Above: Although Khmer Rouge forces had put Phnom Penh under a virtual state of siege by the end of 1973, supplies were still able to reach the Cambodian capital until March 1975. Below: The aftermath of a savage Khmer Rouge attack in Phnom Penh.

Top and above: The fall of Phnom Penh – Khmer Rouge troops parade through the streets of the capital. By 1975 the Khmer Rouge was a well-trained force, armed here with Type-56 assault rifles and RPG-7 rocket launchers.

Phnom Penh remained in government hands and early in January 1974 the Khmer Rouge were within range to shell the capital. Making no attempt to take Phnom Penh by storm, however, the Khmer Rouge contented themselves with imposing a slow stranglehold over the city throughout 1974.

The tempo of events began to increase in the spring of 1975 as North Vietnam mounted its final offensive against the South. In Cambodia it was clear that it would only be a matter of time before Phnom Penh fell to the Khmer Rouge. On 1 April, Lon Nol fled Cambodia, on the 13th the airport at Phnom Penh was closed by artillery fire and on the 17th the communists took control of the city. The country was renamed Democratic Kampuchea and the Khmer Rouge began a reign of terror, exterminating all who in any way seemed to pose a threat to the new regime.

The reckoning for America

Viewed in retrospect American involvement in Laos and Cambodia was an undoubted failure. Despite isolated military victories the American forces were as unable to prevent the expansion of communism in Laos and Cambodia as they had been in South Vietnam.

On the level of high policy, American planners were generally so myopically anti-communist that they failed to perceive the benefits they could have gained from giving active support to the neutralists. Instead, they were too concerned with subverting the neutralist governments in the attempt to replace them with right-wing regimes which, while undoubtedly supporting American short-term objectives, lacked popular support.

Virulent anti-communism similarly blinded the Americans to the knowledge that the whole conflict in Indochina was as much one of nationalism as of ideology. Certainly, nationalism was the strongest motivating force in the war, a fact that the communists realized, but one the Americans did not. The communists were able to present the Americans as successors to the French – a new colonial power. American attitudes to the Indochinese at all levels tended to support this view, while, on the other hand, the communists convinced the people that they were fighting for them in a war of national liberation. The Americans had lost the war for the hearts and minds of the people before they had even started.

From the military perspective the massive US bombing campaigns were a tragic mistake. They did not stop the communists from operating the Ho Chi Minh Trail, nor did they stop the Viet Cong from using the border regions as sanctuary areas – the two prime objectives of American stategy. Instead, the bombing killed tens of thousands of civilians, destroyed the Laotian and Cambodian village economies and in so doing, drove the hard-pressed peasantry into the hands of the communists.

The communist forces were ruthless and unrelenting; their defeat could only have been brought about by depriving them of the support of the people, and by going out to destroy them in the field through infantry action. This the Americans failed to do.

7. The Fall of the South

As American ground troops were withdrawn from Vietnam, so the nature of the war changed. But the South Vietnamese army proved able to sustain the fight against communist insurgency. When the North Vietnamese army invaded in 1972, the South was shaken but, with the support of American airpower, halted the aggressors. Airpower was used as a sophisticated accurate weapon against the economy and military capacity of the North, and it seemed that an answer had been found to communist pressure. But the optimism was illusory. For the Watergate scandal rocked the American political system and made the US commitment dubious. And then, in 1975, the North launched a new offensive, and South Vietnam faced the crisis alone.

A Huey helicopter scans Vietnamese rice paddies while on patrol near Can Tho.

In the spring of 1971 Le Duan, First Secretary of North Vietnam's ruling Lao Dong party, paid an official visit to Moscow. Despite the inevitable rhetoric of fraternal greetings, he was a worried man. The war in the South had reached something of a stalemate since the Tet Offensive of 1968, and although the Hanoi government expressed few doubts about eventual victory, it was obvious that a new strategic approach was needed. Le Duan's mission was to discuss the problem and to solicit Soviet aid in its solution.

The picture which he presented to Moscow was, at first glance, a gloomy one. Since the late 1950s, when military action had been initiated against the Saigon authorities, the aim had been to develop a 'People's War', based upon political subversion, guerrilla attacks and a gradual wearing down of South Vietnamese and, latterly, American resolve. In certain respects this had been successful: by 1968 American domestic opinion had begun to doubt the value of continued military involvement in South-east Asia, significant areas of rural South Vietnam were under the effective control of Viet Cong cadres, backed by troops and supplies from the North, and Saigon politics had devolved into chaos. American combat forces may have been able to contain North Vietnamese incursions into the South and had certainly proved capable of inflicting casualties whenever battle was joined, but with political subversion continuing in the villages behind them, such efforts had been largely negated. Many South Vietnamese peasants, faced with the reality of the Viet Cong presence, had virtually accepted the inevitability of communist victory.

Viet Cong losses

The Tet Offensive of 1968 had changed all this. Politically it may have paid dividends – after all, American casualties and public disquiet about the nature of the war had forced President Johnson to grant important concessions and helped to ensure the election of a new president, intent upon American withdrawal from Vietnam – but militarily it had weakened the communist cause. Irreplaceable Viet Cong units had been withdrawn from rural areas and destroyed in the battles for the provincial capitals, creating a political vacuum which the South Vietnamese had been able to fill, using their American-sponsored 'Pacification' campaign. Most importantly, the myth of Viet Cong invincibility had been shattered. As a result large areas of South Vietnam had entered a period of comparative calm and the writ of the Saigon government had gradually spread into the countryside. By 1971 communist-inspired unrest was apparent in only 10 of the country's 45 provinces, potentially affecting less than a quarter of the population, and reports of armed clashes between the Army of the Republic of South Vietnam (ARVN) and the Viet Cong had declined significantly. If a 'People's War' was the road to communist victory, such evidence suggested that subversive cadres in the South would have to be rebuilt, using 'fillers' from the North Vietnamese Army.

The new strategic option

But there was an alternative, based upon a slightly more optimistic analysis. In line with President Nixon's election pledge, by 1971 American ground forces had been drastically reduced in South Vietnam from the all-time high of 542,000 in January 1969 to little over 225,000, and further reductions were in the immediate pipeline. They had been replaced by a process of 'Vietnamization', with corresponding increases to the strength of the ARVN, but this had caused problems. With ARVN desertion rates reportedly running at the staggering level of 100,000 a year, a general lack of technical training among the soldiers and a persistent weakness in overall South Vietnamese resolve, the nation's security was by no means guaranteed even when the paper strength of its entire armed forces topped the one million mark. In addition, although American air potential remained theoretically available to the Saigon government, it was not improbable to argue that American public opinion would restrict its full commitment in time of crisis. All this suggested to the North Vietnamese that a full-scale conventional invasion of the South, delivered before Vietnamization had been properly established, might provide the means to swift and easy victory.

This was the proposal which Le Duan took to Moscow, together with a request for military aid. The Soviets were impressed. With an American presidential election due in 1972, further problems in South Vietnam would be sure to embarrass Nixon and might even lead to his

Opposite above: South Vietnamese Rangers prepare to be airlifted to the battlezone. Opposite below: A wounded Viet Cong prisoner is brought in for questioning. Above: A dead soldier of the North Vietnamese Army lies by the roadside after an unsuccessful raid on a US Marine position. Right: While a comrade stands guard, a South Vietnamese Marine absentmindedly tries his hand at the organ during fighting in Saigon in 1968.

Above: A North Vietnamese artillery officer in a typically well camouflaged position. Below: Men of the NVA march to the front, armed with rocket launchers.

political defeat, while a unified Vietnam, indebted to Moscow for aid, would act as a useful counter to the power of China in South-east Asia. They agreed to help. Throughout the rest of 1971 massive deliveries of arms flowed into Haiphong. By the turn of the year the NVA had been transformed into a potentially powerful conventional force, equipped with T54, T34, and PT76 tanks, SAM delivery systems, modern artillery pieces and a fleet of heavy trucks. The Ho Chi Minh Trail, winding down from North Vietnam through the border areas of Laos and Cambodia to the South, was widened to cope with increased traffic, new roads were built up to and into the Demilitarized Zone (DMZ) and supply dumps were established at key points close to intended invasion routes. General Vo Nguyen Giap, architect of Viet Minh victory against the French in the 1950s and hero of Dien Bien Phu, took overall command, intent on overthrowing the government of President Nguyen Van Thieu by force of arms.

Communist conventional warfare

Giap's strategy was a complex one. Instead of concentrating his considerable force – estimated to number some 200,000 men with full armour and artillery support – in a single all-out attack, he divided it into three separate thrusts many miles apart. The main assault was to be delivered in the northern provinces of Quang Tri and Thua Thien, where significant ARVN forces were concentrated, with NVA divisions moving southwards through the DMZ and eastwards along the A Shau valley from Laos. Their aim was to encircle and destroy ARVN units around Quang Tri City and Hué, capturing the two northern provinces and emasculating South Vietnamese military power. At the same time NVA troops, in conjunction with surviving Viet Cong cadres, were to advance out of southern Cambodia into the provinces of Tay Ninh and Binh Long, threatening Saigon and tying down ARVN reserves. Finally a third attack, exploiting ARVN over-stretch, was to drive out of eastern Cambodia towards Kontum in the Central Highlands before linking up with infiltration units in the coastal province of Binh Dinh and splitting South Vietnam in half. Faced with such disasters, Thieu would be forced to surrender. The plan had the obvious merit of spreading the enemy out, but it ignored the possibility of piecemeal NVA defeat and took little account of the potential impact of American and South Vietnamese air strikes against the exposed communist attackers.

In fact air power affected the offensive even before it began, for as early as December 1971 American reconnaissance aircraft picked up the signs of NVA activity in the border areas. Selected strikes, carried out largely by South Vietnamese pilots, hit supply dumps and force concentrations throughout January and February, disrupting NVA movement and probably delaying the start of an offensive which had been widely expected to coincide with the Tet celebrations. However, as Tet passed without incident, South Vietnamese units relaxed their guard. When the assault eventually began, under cover of poor weather, in the early hours of Good Friday, 30 March 1972, a substantial degree of tactical surprise was achieved.

This paved the way for an initial run of NVA successes, particularly in the northern provinces where three NVA divisions, backed by 200 tanks and large numbers of 130mm artillery pieces, swept forward in their two-pronged attack. In Quang Tri the ARVN 3rd Division bore

Above: A North Vietnamese heavy machine gun fitted with rudimentary anti-aircraft sights. Above right: A North Vietnamese mortar team in action. Right: The North Vietnamese invasion of the South in 1972 marked a change from guerrilla to conventional warfare.

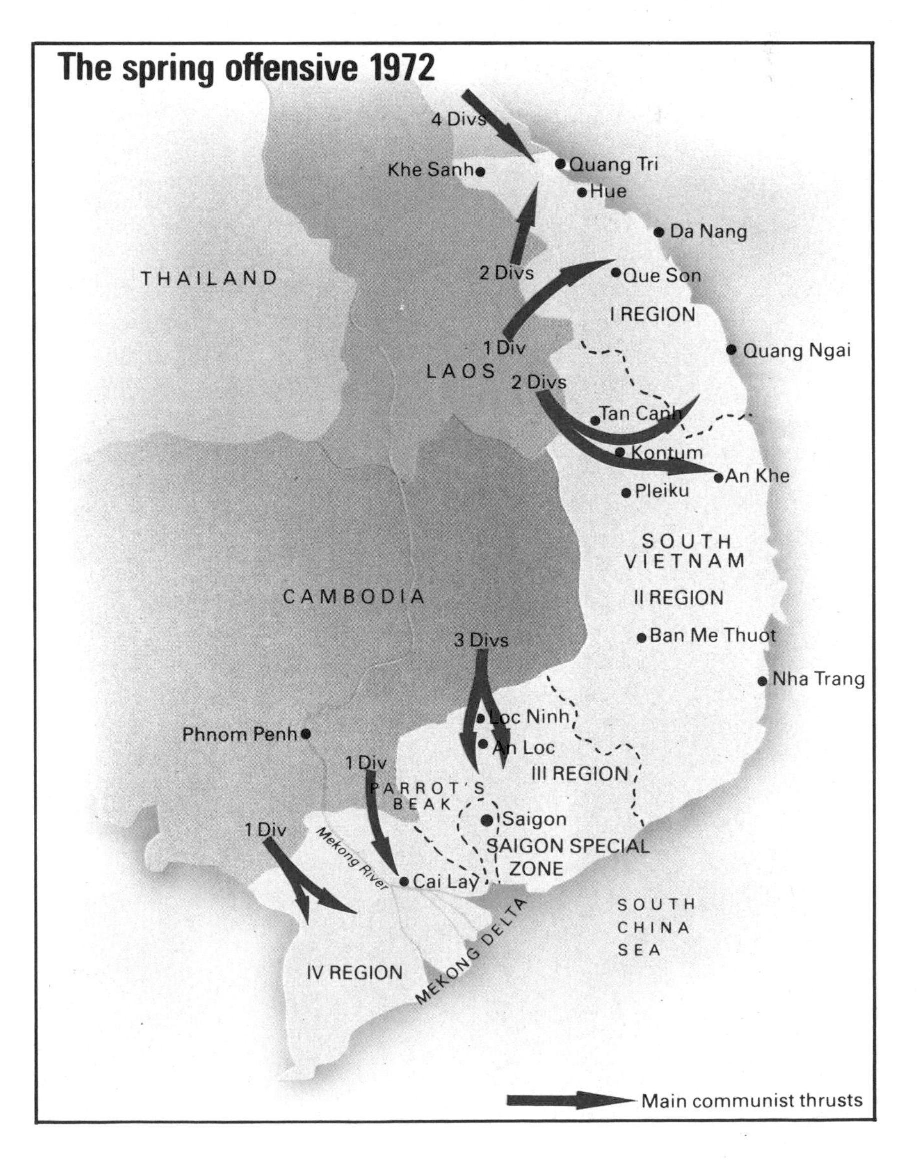

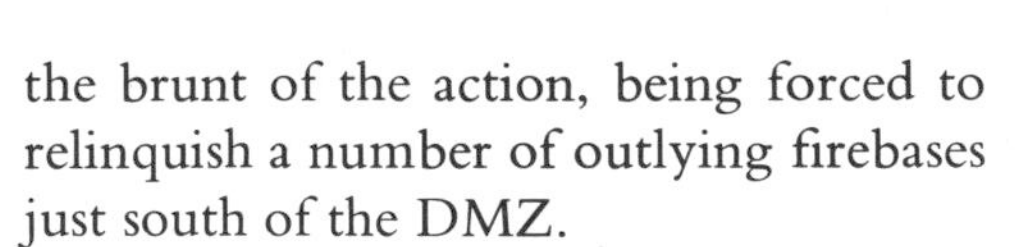

the brunt of the action, being forced to relinquish a number of outlying firebases just south of the DMZ.

Their task was made more difficult by a complete absence of air support until the weather began to clear in early April, and although by then an extemporized defence line had been established on the Cua Viet River, a strip of territory 10 miles (16 km) deep had been lost. Further south, in Thua Thien, a similar picture emerged as ARVN forces pulled back down the A Shau valley to protect the approaches to Hué, for it was not until April, when Nixon authorized the release of American aircraft (including B-52s) for close-support missions, that a defence line could be set up. By the middle of the

month the NVA had succeeded in taking valuable territory and inflicting considerable casualties, but they had been stopped, principally by a series of air-strikes which, at times, took place only yards away from front-line ARVN positions.

South Vietnam's reaction

But this was only part of the NVA offensive, and if the aim of the other two thrusts was to tie down South Vietnamese reserves, it was certainly achieved. As news of the attacks in the north filtered through to Saigon, Thieu was unable to devote his full attention to the crisis, for simultaneously the threat to his capital developed. On 2 April the NVA moved into Tay Ninh, overwhelming isolated outposts and pushing ARVN units back towards Saigon. Reserves were rushed to the area, only to discover that this was a ruse, as the main weight of the enemy advance shifted suddenly to the neighbouring province of Binh Long. On 6 April the ARVN firebase at Loc Ninh

was overrun, despite a concentration of 'close-in' air support, and NVA troops approached the town of An Loc, astride Highway 13 – a direct route to Saigon. Thieu had no choice but to react, reinforcing An Loc with an airborne brigade and ordering the 21st Division to the area. The town was soon besieged, coming under sustained ground attack from 13 April, and it was only through the commitment of American fighter-bombers and B-52s that the perimeter held. Ten days later the third arm of the NVA strategy emerged as the ARVN 22nd Division fell back in disarray towards Kontum and towns in Binh Dinh province came under attack. Once again, South Vietnamese reserves were committed, American air strikes were authorized and, by the end of April, Kontum was under siege.

By this time the ARVN was stretched to the limits and although some comfort could be gleaned from the fact that all three NVA assaults had been blunted, such a state of affairs could not be expected to last. Nor did it, for on 27 April the NVA resumed their northern offensive, concentrating against the 3rd Division in Quang Tri. Under massive artillery and tank attacks and without hope of reinforcement, the formation broke, streaming back to Dong Ha and Quang Tri City in panic. By 1 May Quang Tri province was under virtual NVA control and the panic was spreading rapidly to the defenders of Hué as soldiers and civilians fled south along Highway 1 under sustained NVA artillery fire which, it has been estimated, inflicted over 20,000 casualties. It began to look as if Giap's strategy was working.

Thieu regains control

But he had reckoned without continued American support for the Saigon government, manifested not only in the form of air-strikes but also in the commitment of all available vessels of the 7th Fleet, which bombarded NVA positions on the northern front throughout the period of crisis. This undoubtedly reinforced South Vietnamese resolve. On 2 May Thieu dismissed the regional commander of the northern provinces, replacing him with General Ngo Quang Truong, a trusted and highly competent officer. He quickly reimposed order around Hué – chiefly by threatening to execute deserters and looters – and established a new defensive line about 25 miles (40 km) north of the city. Fortunately he had at his disposal the Marine and 1st Divisions – veteran formations which had been largely unaffected by the panic – and they held firm. The NVA, delayed by the tide of refugees they had themselves created and suffering under both sea and air bombardment, could not maintain the momentum of advance, exposing a basic flaw in Giap's plan. Although he had succeeded in spreading his enemy out, he had in the process divided his own forces between three widely separated areas of attack with no central reserve available to exploit success. So long as Hué, An Loc and Kontum held out, the ARVN could defeat the invasion.

This is, in fact, what happened, although not without some exceptionally fierce fighting in all three areas. At An Loc the defenders came under intense attack until 12 May and only survived a final assault by seven regiments when B-52s hit the NVA concentration areas. At Kontum the situation was no different: NVA attacks were beaten off in house-to-house fighting which lasted until the end

Opposite above: An Loc after the NVA offensive. Opposite below: An F-4 Phantom, a powerful fighter bomber that did much to aid ARVN ground forces. Below: An ARVN soldier takes a light from a comrade during a lull in the fighting. Bottom: South Vietnamese villagers watch an American air strike on a suspected communist position.

of May – at one point American aircraft even had to bomb the town itself to prevent a breakthrough. Only at Hué, where the NVA had been weakened in their advance, was a close siege avoided, but it was not until late June – by which time units released from the Kontum battle were available as reinforcements – that ARVN counter-offensive operations could begin. By that time the NVA had been badly mauled, enabling the South Vietnamese to recover some of the territory so recently lost. Even so, this took until the end of the year and did not succeed in restoring the full *status quo ante bellum*: at the time of the ceasefire in January 1973 the NVA still occupied a strip of territory to the south of the DMZ as well as bases in many border provinces.

North Vietnam's defeat

The North Vietnamese invasion, costing an estimated 100,000 lives, had therefore failed to achieve its objectives and in retrospect it is not difficult to see why. Giap's plan contained the basic flaw of dividing instead of concentrating his available force, South Vietnamese resolve was underestimated and, most importantly of all, the full impact of American commitment was not taken into account. Without that commitment it is not unreasonable to suppose that the ARVN would have collapsed by early May, for in the battles for all three areas under attack it was American weapons which turned the tide. In the north it was the 7th Fleet which provided almost unlimited fire support, delivering a total of 16,100 tons of explosives onto North Vietnamese positions between April and September, but even that would have been insufficient to guarantee ARVN success without the concurrent use of air power. This was the key to victory, for if Nixon had not authorized its release on 2 April, An Loc and Kontum would certainly have fallen and the defence of Hué would probably never have been established. Close-support missions – 74 per cent of which were flown by American pilots – succeeded in destroying NVA tanks, artillery positions and force concentrations wherever they could

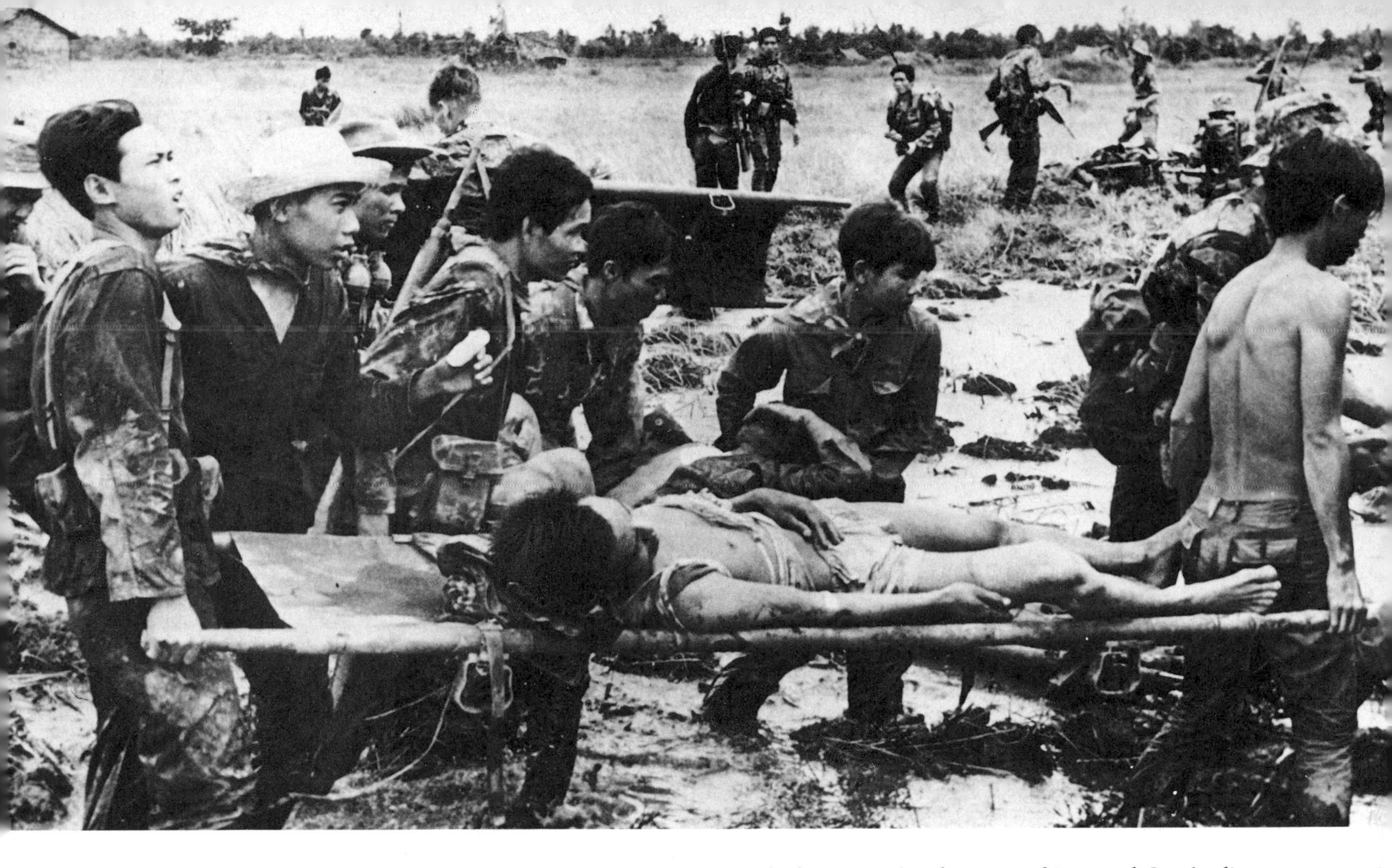

Opposite above: Refugees flee from the advancing North Vietnamese while one family hides in a water culvert. Opposite below: South Vietnamese troops in action – the spring offensive of 1972 was a testing ground for the ARVN.
Above: ARVN troops remove their wounded from the battlefield. Below: A Vought A-7 Corsair attack bomber prepares for launch aboard the aircraft carrier USS Constellation.

be found, inflicting losses which were decisive. The B-52s – each of which was capable of delivering over 30 tons of bombs – were particularly effective, covering the weaknesses of ARVN units by acting as their artillery support. It was an expensive way of doing things, but it did work. At the same time, air reconnaissance provided warning and information, supply aircraft sustained the garrisons at An Loc and Kontum and the ubiquitous helicopters provided mobility and gunship support. It was a formidable package.

Strategic bombing

Nor was this the full extent of American air commitment in 1972, for while such tactical support developed, Nixon exerted more direct pressure on Hanoi through strategic bombing. Air attacks against the North had, of course, been used before under the operational name of *Rolling Thunder,* but these had been stopped on 31 October 1968 as part of the *quid pro quo* for North Vietnamese involvement in the Paris peace talks, and had not been resumed on a regular basis. Raids against NVA or Viet Cong strongholds in the border areas of Laos and Cambodia were still carried out, particularly in late 1971 and early 1972 as signs of the pre-invasion build-up appeared, but missions north of the DMZ were tightly controlled. Between November 1968 and April 1972 the only permitted air activity over North Vietnam consisted of unarmed reconnaissance flights, although whenever they were fired on Nixon did order 'protective reaction strikes' against enemy air defences. Such constraint undoubtedly produced military disadvantages – many American commanders argued that an early resumption of bombing could have prevented the 1972 invasion – but it did provide Nixon with a useful 'tool of persuasion' when the invasion began.

He did not hesitate to use it. On 2 April American aircraft were authorized to cross the DMZ to a depth of 25 miles (40 km), hitting supply dumps and lines of communication as part of their interdiction campaign against the NVA, and these operations, known collectively as *Freedom Train,* were extended to the 19th and then to the 20th parallel as the ground war intensified. The main aim was to cut the NVA off from its supply

Above: US Navy pilots describe their exploits in shooting down a Mig-17. Below: The mining of the sea lanes around North Vietnam proved a highly successful operation. Opposite above: North Vietnamese bystanders survey the ruins brought about by an American bombing attack on Hanoi. Opposite below left: One of the most impressive uses of US military technology was the laser or television-guided 'smart' bombs. Opposite below right: A North Vietnamese anti-aircraft position. By the early seventies the communists had developed a comprehensive air defence system that included conventional artillery and radar-guided surface-to-air missiles.

bases in the North, but other advantages did emerge. South Vietnamese morale was clearly boosted at a critical time, helping to produce the resolve which contributed to military victory, and a useful 'bargaining chip' was introduced to the flagging peace talks in Paris. If the North Vietnamese refused to discuss a ceasefire, Nixon could extend the scope of the bombing; if they showed signs of conciliation he could reduce it or call a halt.

Cutting off supplies

This is exactly what he did. By early May, with the NVA offensive making significant gains, the Paris talks bogged down and Nixon increased the aerial pressure. On 8 May, in an unprecedented move designed to cut the North Vietnamese off from their sources of outside supply, he authorized the mining of Haiphong and other northern ports, ordered a blockade of the coast and released the bombers over the whole of the North except for a narrow buffer zone close to the Chinese border. Some of the restrictions of *Rolling Thunder* were relaxed – presidential authorization was only needed when industrial targets actually in Hanoi or Haiphong were to be attacked, otherwise local commanders could decide for themselves when and what on a target list to hit – and more effective weapons, including the extremely accurate 'Smart' bombs, were deployed.

The campaign, code-named *Linebacker,* continued until late October, achieving impressive results. Over 40,000 individual aircraft sorties were flown, delivering 155,000 tons of bombs, and a whole series of crucial targets, including key bridges, airfields, power plants and munitions storage facilities, were destroyed. The North Vietnamese, already facing defeat in the South, found that few supplies were getting through the blockade and that what was available could not be delivered to their forces in the field along shattered lines of communication. The official American estimate is that the supply flow to the NVA was reduced by *Linebacker* to between 35 and 50 per cent of the pre-invasion figures. Small wonder, therefore, that the Hanoi government thought it prudent to make concessions at the Paris talks, enabling Nixon to halt the campaign on 23 October.

Linebacker II

Unfortunately this proved to be a premature move, for the North Vietnamese used the respite to resume their former intransigence and the talks broke down yet again. On 19 December Nixon reacted by ordering a resumption of the bombing under the unofficial code-name *Linebacker II,* but by now his aims had changed. It was no longer necessary to bolster up ARVN military efforts in the South – by December the NVA had been pushed back on all fronts – nor even to boost South Vietnamese morale, but it was politically desirable to procure a ceasefire which would allow for an honourable American withdrawal in line with Nixon's re-election pledge. *Linebacker II* was therefore an attempt to force the North Vietnamese to a settlement through punitive air action, involving a short, intensive bombing campaign against war-related targets. It was devastatingly successful, for in a 12-day period (19-30 December 1972) a total of 729 B-52 and over 1000 fighter-bomber sorties were flown over all areas of the North, with special attention being devoted to industrial targets in the Hanoi/Haiphong complex. Over 20,000 tons of bombs were dropped, destroying rail yards, electrical power plants, internal communications, airfields and air defence systems. The cost was not particularly high – 26 American aircraft failed to

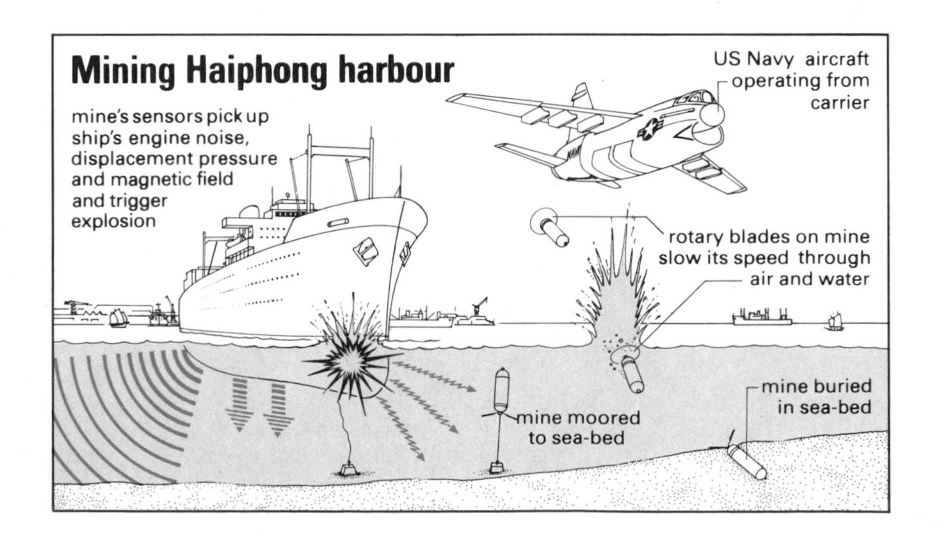

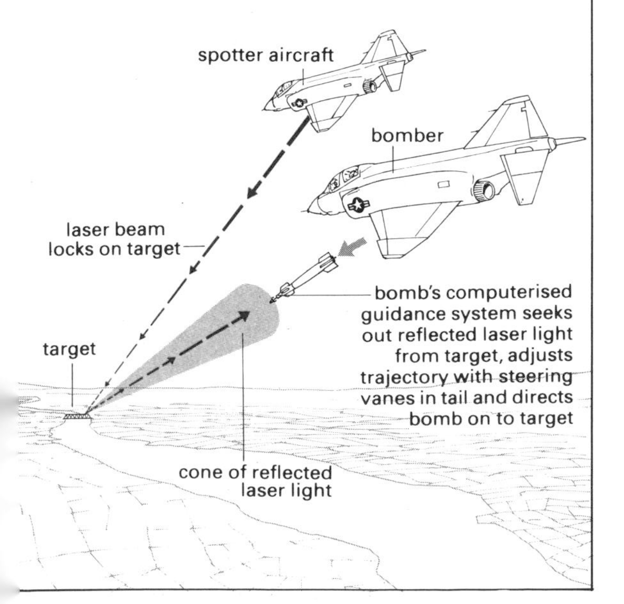

ne 'smart' laser-guided bomb
spotter aircraft
bomber
laser beam
locks on target
bomb's computerised
guidance system seeks
out reflected laser light
from target, adjusts
trajectory with steering
vanes in tail and directs
bomb on to target
target
cone of reflected
laser light

Top: Members of the North Vietnamese Peoples' Militia return to work after an American air raid. Above: An infantryman of the ARVN stands guard before an impending Viet Cong attack. Grenade-launchers – such as the one shown here – were widely used in the fighting in Vietnam.

return, including 15 B-52s – and the North Vietnamese, faced with the imminent destruction of their economy and war-making capability, soon made it known that they were prepared to resume negotiations. On 30 December Nixon halted the bombing and on 1 January 1973 the Paris talks reopened in a new atmosphere of conciliation. By 9 January a ceasefire had been agreed in principle and 12 days later it was initialled by US National Security Adviser Henry Kissinger and North Vietnam's chief negotiator Le Duc Tho. It marked the end of direct American involvement in the Vietnam War.

Peace with honour

The fact that this was Nixon's main aim is reflected in the terms of the agreement, most of which were geared primarily to an 'honourable' American withdrawal, with little thought as to the long-term security of South Vietnam. Thus, although it was laid down that all 'foreign troops' would leave the country forthwith, the existence of a separate clause establishing an 'in-place' ceasefire restricted this in reality to an American withdrawal only. NVA troops who were still occupying territory to the south of the Demilitarized Zone as well as in the western and southern provinces of South Vietnam remained *in situ*, conveniently poised for future 'land grabs' or incursions, and actually controlling about five per cent of the South's population. Moreover, any attempt by the ARVN to recapture such territory would be in breach of the ceasefire, all violations of which were to be monitored by a special International Commission for Control and Supervision. Unfortunately, as this body contained representatives from countries which were friendly towards Hanoi, similar restraints upon NVA actions could not be guaranteed.

Not surprisingly the Saigon government did its best to oppose these terms but Nixon, convinced that they were the only ones available and intent upon satisfying public demands for an end to American involvement, insisted upon their acceptance. Even so, he was obliged to make promises, both oral and written, that American air power would be made available to the South if the NVA attacked again and to guarantee continued economic support for the maintenance and improvement of South Vietnam's armed forces. It was only when this had been made clear that Thieu, with extreme reluctance, agreed to the ceasefire.

South Vietnam alone

In retrospect South Vietnamese misgivings were more than justified, for as the months went by the prospects for a lasting peace deteriorated and the security of South Vietnam declined. The main reason for this was what appeared to be a gradual American abandonment of the country. Despite the promises made to Thieu in January 1973, material aid to the South Vietnamese armed forces was not delivered in quantities sufficient to maintain effectiveness. Much of the equipment provided was secondhand (F-5 aircraft, for example, were delivered from South Korea and Taiwan rather than American stockpiles) and spares were in short supply. More importantly, the requested financial aid, so essential to a country which lay shattered from the effects of more than a decade of war, was progressively cut by American politicians intent upon preventing renewed involvement at any level in South-east Asia. In 1974, for example, the military aid package was summarily reduced by Congress from an expected 1.6 billion to 700 million dollars and all requests for additional aid were refused. At the same time, as Nixon came under increasing pressure from the Watergate scandal, even political commitment to the protection of South Vietnam declined. America began to look inwards, absorbed by domestic events, and although the promise of air power support was renewed by President Ford when he replaced the discredited Nixon in August 1974, it should have been obvious that he no longer enjoyed the freedom of action required.

This placed the Saigon government in an impossible position. On the one hand they recognized the need for American support and believed quite logically that the heavy sacrifices made by that nation to prevent communist expansion before 1973 gave her a vested interest in the continued independence of South Vietnam; on the other they were forced to accept the results of growing American disillusionment and introspection. The fact that Thieu and his ministers clung to the belief that, in the event of another invasion, the B-52s would reappear to save Saigon, is an indication of their desperation.

Thieu's isolation

But there was more to it than this, for even if American support had been forthcoming there is ample evidence to suggest that South Vietnam was itself incapable of long-term survival. The political structure of the state was corrupt and inefficient with Thieu becoming progressively more unpopular and isolated from reality. Many of his ministers and local administrators seemed to be more intent upon lining their pockets than dealing with the enormous political, economic and military problems of their country. One of Thieu's closest advisers, General Dan Van Quong, head of the National Security Committee, was widely known as 'Fat Quong' for his black-market dealings in rice and opium, and he was merely one of the more flamboyant examples of a general malaise which sapped South Vietnamese resolve. In the sort of war being waged by the North, where the aim was political power rather than simple military victory, the Saigon government could not afford to lose contact with its people, yet this was exactly what was happening.

The middle classes and peasants were the ones being asked to pay for national security in terms of lives, money and property, but were presented with a ruling clique who cared little and did even less. In such circumstances, although few people openly supported the North Vietnamese cause (they had made too many sacrifices already to go that far), they became indifferent and apathetic towards their own government, creating a political vacuum in the state which the NVA and its political cadres were more than willing to fill.

Nor was the situation helped by a steady decline in the effectiveness of the South Vietnamese armed forces. They were ill-prepared both psychologically and materially to stand against the NVA once the Americans withdrew, for they had grown used to American primacy in all aspects of security. At the strategic level the Military Assistance Command Vietnam (MACV), headed by an American general and backed by all the intelligence-gathering facilities and resources of a Superpower, had virtually decided how, where and when the war was to be

Above: Indonesian and Iranian officers of the ICCS investigate a breach of the 1973 ceasefire – a VC sapper attack on a South Vietnamese outpost. Below: One of the many graveyards in South Vietnam. Although no completely accurate figures can be given it has been estimated that around 400,000 South Vietnamese died during the war.

Above: North Vietnamese artillerymen load a shell into a heavy field gun. Below: A South Vietnamese gunner takes a break from the rigours of war.

fought, precluding the need for a professional South Vietnamese General Staff. When the last of the MACV personnel were withdrawn from Saigon in 1973, therefore, Thieu faced the prospect of continuing the conflict without access to expert advice. South Vietnamese strategic thinking was stultified and weak, being based in the end almost entirely upon the rather vain hope that the B-52s would arrive in time.

It was the same at the organizational and tactical levels, for although Vietnamization had been introduced as early as 1967, the process had been slow and was still far from complete by 1973. South Vietnamese troops were not well-suited to the American methods of warfare which they inherited – indeed those very methods, inapplicable to the geography and strategic situation of South Vietnam, constituted a major problem in their own right – and were put into poorly organized models of Western units in what was essentially a Far Eastern war. The vast majority were unwilling conscripts, called up for unlimited periods of service and devoid of the technical training needed to operate and repair equipment left behind by the Americans. Moreover, the draft was notoriously unjust, subject to the corruption which permeated South Vietnamese society, and as a result desertion was endemic, regularly running at levels which could not be cancelled out even with an annual intake of 120,000 recruits. To cover such losses, while at the same time making money, some unit commanders turned to yet more corruption, packing their muster-rolls with 'ghost soldiers' who did not in fact exist but to whom pay was still afforded. According to one report on the situation in the Mekong Delta military region in early 1975, no less than 30,000 such 'ghost soldiers' existed in a force of 150,000.

Crisis for the South

But even if full strength could have been achieved, the forces were unlikely to be effective, modelled as they were upon a sophisticated American war-machine which the state could not afford to maintain. South Vietnam, in common with many other countries in the early 1970s, suffered the ravages of inflation, and as the price of military equipment rose, less and less money – in real terms – could be devoted to defence. Fuel was a particular problem, for the price of oil quadrupled on world markets in the aftermath of the 1973 Arab-Israeli War and, as South Vietnam had no indigenous supply, she could not afford to maintain her military stocks. As a result, ARVN units no longer enjoyed unlimited access to trucks and helicopters for transport and rapidly lost their mobility, while the air force was directed to restrict its flying time, something which affected not only the provision of air support to ground units but also the training of new pilots. Indeed by 1975 11 of the original 66 South Vietnamese squadrons had been completely disbanded. A similar picture emerged over ammunition, for as the price rose the stockpiles dwindled, in some cases to less than 20 per cent of their 1972 levels, and the firepower which had been such a characteristic of American tactics virtually disappeared.

Inevitably all of this deeply affected morale at every level of South Vietnamese society, undermining the advantages gained from the victory of 1972 and leaving the state extremely vulnerable to renewed enemy pressure. On paper the armed forces may have been strong – in early 1975 they comprised 55 airforce squadrons, 11 infantry divisions, one Marine and one Airborne division, some Ranger and armoured units and a substantial number of Regional and Popular Forces, totalling some 1.1 million men – but their weaknesses were enormous. They were declining in effectiveness, defending an insecure base and supporting a corrupt and inefficient political leadership.

North Vietnamese build-up

By comparison the NVA had not wasted the respite provided by the ceasefire. Despite their lack of success in 1972, the North Vietnamese continued to receive substantial Soviet aid, enabling them to rebuild their military strength and prepare for a fresh offensive from bases which still existed in the South. The Ho Chi

Above: Members of the South Vietnamese Peoples' Self-Defense Force receive instruction in hamlet defence. Opposite above: The forces of the ARVN were overwhelmed by the 1975 communist offensive. Opposite below: NVA soldiers on top of a Soviet-built T55.

Minh Trail, now free from American air interdiction, was improved and a new road network built through the mountains on the Laotian and Cambodian borders. POL (Petrol, Oil, Lubricant) pipelines were pushed as far forward as possible to ensure a steady supply of trucks and tanks, creating a potential for sustained conventional warfare, and SAM defences were established to prevent disruption of the build-up. By late 1974 a total of 19 NVA divisions, fully manned and stocked, were available, 12 of them actually in the South, and the pressure was gradually stepped up.

In fact the pressure had never been turned off, for since the ceasefire the NVA had conducted a continuous campaign of harassment and expansion, particularly in the northern provinces. Bitter fighting had flared up in 1974 – the ARVN lost an estimated 15,000 casualties in Quang Nam province alone, protecting the approaches to Danang – and this had led to a 'top heavy' deployment of South Vietnamese units. A total of five ARVN divisions, including the Marine and Airborne, were concentrated in the north by early 1975, leaving the rest of the country only sparsely defended. This suited the NVA. Aware of the enormous problems facing the South and convinced that America would not react,

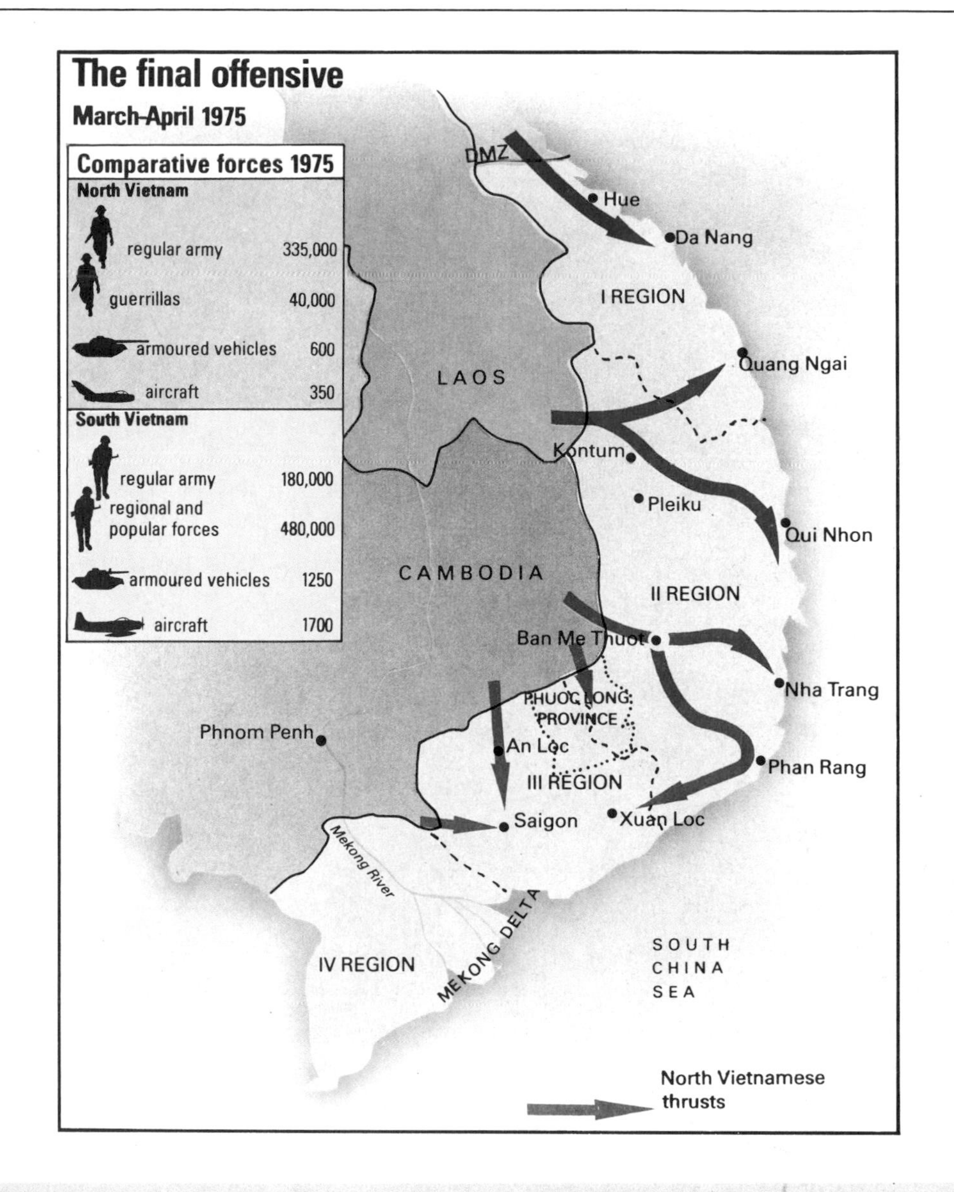

a strategy of gradual encroachment was introduced, designed to tie down ARVN units in the north while grabbing territory elsewhere. The first indications of this became apparent in January 1975 when the thinly-defended province of Phuoc Long, to the north-east of Saigon, was attacked. Thieu was caught unawares, without strong reserves, and although he did order heliborne Rangers to be committed they could not prevent the loss of the entire province. Significantly, the Americans did not react.

A general offensive

The North Vietnamese now saw just how vulnerable Thieu was, and while the battle for Phuoc Long was continuing the Hanoi Politburo authorized a more general offensive, designed to wear down ARVN strength preparatory to total victory in 1976. Appointing General Van Tien Dung to command operations, they gathered overwhelming forces for an attack against Ban Me Thuot, capital of Darlac province in the Central Highlands. Intelligence reports had shown this region to be poorly defended, with two ARVN divisions concentrated around Pleiku and Kontum, leaving Ban Me Thuot in the hands of one regiment only. Three NVA divisions moved to isolate the town in early March, laying siege to it with tactics reminiscent of 1972. But there the similarities ended. With little air support and scant hope of reinforcement or supply, the ARVN defenders stood no chance at all. On 10 March the perimeter was breached by armour and infantry attack and within 48 hours the town was in communist hands.

On its own this need not have been disastrous, but Thieu's reaction was extreme. Convinced that his country was about to be split in half, with a substantial part of the army cut off in the northern provinces, he ordered a radical redeployment. The Airborne Division – one of the only truly professional ARVN units – was to be withdrawn to the south, out of danger; the remaining formations in the north were to pull back to the coast in case they needed suddenly to be evacuated by sea; and in the Central Highlands Major-General Pham Van Phu was to withdraw his regular units from Pleiku and Kontum preparatory to the retaking of Ban Me Thuot.

The results were appalling. When Phu gave the necessary orders, panic broke out in Pleiku and Kontum as soldiers and civilians alike interpreted the move as a prelude to communist occupation, and this began a process of rapid and uncontrollable disintegration throughout the Central Highlands. The situation was not eased by the choice of route for withdrawal, for Route 7B, leading to the coast at Tuy Hoa, was in a sad state of disrepair, with vital bridges cut or incapable of taking heavy traffic. The move began on 16 March and should have taken 48 hours, but progress was hampered by a mass of panic-stricken refugees and, inevitably, NVA harassing attacks. The so-called 'Column of Tears' was massacred and although a few of the better-disciplined troops did struggle through to the coast, by 1 April the Central Highlands were in NVA hands. Moreover, as this situation developed, the northern provinces also came under sustained attack, and as the redeployment ordered by Thieu for that region took place, it too fell prey to panic and confusion. Hué fell on 25 March and although plans were made to defend Danang it soon became obvious that this was impracticable. Evacuation was ordered on 29 March, but few ARVN soldiers survived.

The North Vietnamese realized that the time was ripe for an all-out assault on Saigon, a year earlier than anticipated. NVA divisions in the Central Highlands were redeployed, supplies were quickly brought up by road and sea, and ARVN units were pinned to their existing locations by selected preliminary attacks which left Saigon virtually undefended. The 18th Division put up a spirited defence at Xuan Loc, to the east of the city, holding off the NVA advance until 18 April, but their sacrifice was in vain. Thieu ran out of reserves, ideas and strategic options. On 21 April, in an angry broadcast during which he condemned the lack of American aid, he resigned, handing over to General Duong Van Minh ('Big Minh'), a moderate with whom it was hoped the North Vietnamese would negotiate. But they refused to compromise and nine days later, as the Americans conducted a confused and badly organized evacuation of selected personnel, Minh surrendered unconditionally. South Vietnam ceased to exist. As this coincided with similar communist takeovers in Cambodia and Laos, a new era in Indochinese history had begun.

Opposite: As the armies of the NVA pushed further into South Vietnam so many South Vietnamese fled towards the seeming safety of the capital, Saigon. Above: The arrival of communist troops on the outskirts of Saigon caused confusion and panic. Here US Marines repel desperate South Vietnamese civilians attempting to gain sanctuary in the American Embassy. Right: Refugees in Xuan Loc struggle to gain a place aboard a departing helicopter.

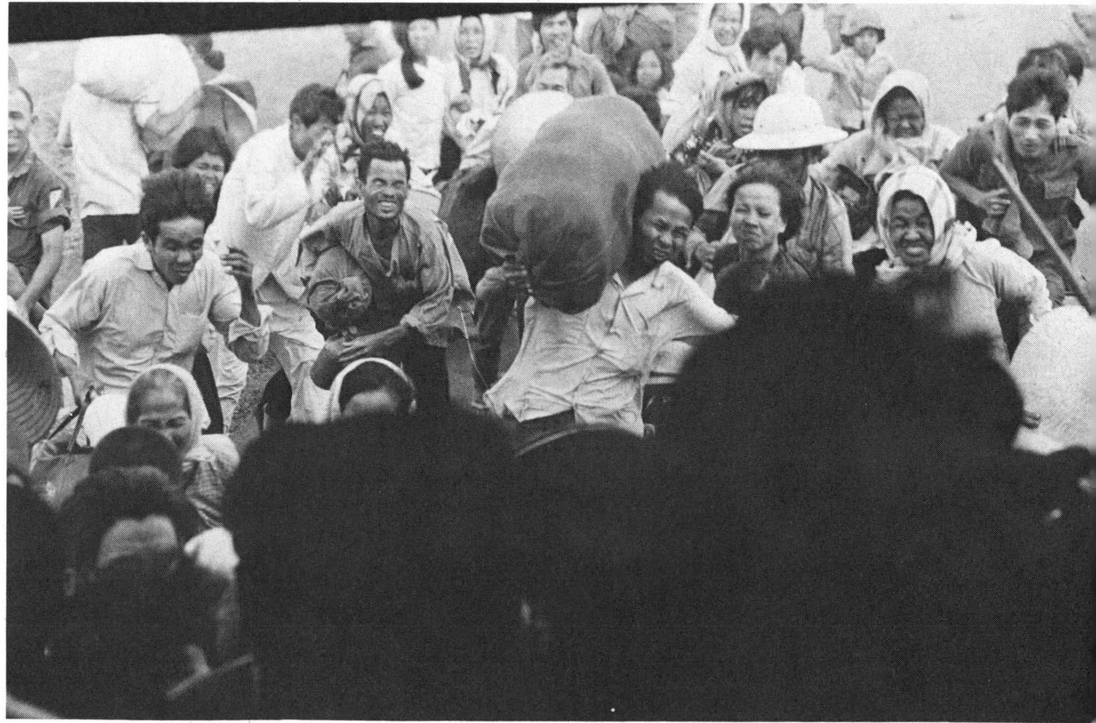

8. The Never-Ending Conflict

Victory for the communists in South Vietnam was not the end of Indochina's troubles; it was merely the prelude to a series of wars and political struggles that continued to shatter the life of the civilian population. In Vietnam itself, forcible socialization led to the flight of many Chinese – the so-called boat people – while in Laos, fighting continued. The greatest misery was in Cambodia, where Pol Pot's Khmer Rouge regime caused untold deaths, and provoked an invasion by the Vietnamese, who in their occupation of Cambodia became themselves the target of a guerrilla war that spread as far as Thailand. And then, in 1979, the Chinese also entered the tangled politics of Indochina with a punitive invasion of Vietnam.

Vietnamese recruits undergo training in preparation for the invasion of Cambodia in 1978. Despite Vietnamese claims that they were merely aiding Cambodian communists in their fight against Pol Pot's regime, the Vietnamese Army was the direct instrument in bringing about the overthrow of the Khmer Rouge in Cambodia.

The wars in Indochina between 1945 and 1975 probably cost in excess of three million lives. Communist victory in Laos, Cambodia and Vietnam has not, however, brought an end to the suffering both because of the internal implications of that victory for each state and through the re-emergence of traditional rivalries in Indochina. It was in this context that the prime minister of Singapore, Lee Kuan Yew, spoke in January 1979 of the region's thousands of refugees as 'victims of peace'.

The fall of Phnom Penh to the Khmer Rouge on 17 April 1975 and of Saigon to the North Vietnamese 13 days later, as well as the consolidation of communist power in Laos by December 1975, brought immediate retribution for the supporters of the defeated governments. In Vietnam there were undoubtedly some summary executions while all former officials and soldiers of the Thieu government were required to register. Prominent supporters were committed to *Trai Cai Tao* (re-education camps) where they were subjected to a harsh regime of hard labour, inadequate food and indoctrination lectures and discussions. It is estimated that 200,000 persons were interned in 50 camps by 1977 and it is possible that as many as 50,000 remain there although the Vietnamese claimed in March 1978 that 90 per cent had been released. Less important officials and soldiers were given re-education sessions in schools or halls while the southern population as a whole has been exposed to propaganda ranging from the official newspaper, *Giai Phong*, to new school textbooks. The population has also been closely supervised with 'people's revolutionary committees' down to village level and 'solidarity cells' of between 10 and 20 families to facilitate surveillance. Major religions such as Buddhism and Catholicism have been persecuted while some sects such as the Cao Dai and Hoa Hao are believed to have forcibly resisted the communists in the Mekong Delta and Central Highlands. Equally, there have been campaigns against Western culture, clothes and long hair.

Socialist transformation

Another feature of communist rule in Vietnam has been the concepts of 'socialist construction' and 'socialist transformation'. The Five Year Plan announced in December 1976 emphasized the planned relocation of the urban population of the South in rural areas. Some 700,000 people had been forced to leave Saigon (renamed Ho Chi Minh City in July 1976) by June 1977 for the 'new economic zones' and a total of 1.3 million relocated by January 1978. The project has been marred by natural disasters and mismanagement while the population, organized into 'production groups', has suffered from food and housing shortages and rampant disease. Some private enterprise was allowed to survive until the government announced in March 1978 that it intended to switch the entrepreneurial classes to 'production'. The introduction of a new currency involving a 90 per cent devaluation in September 1975 had already effectively eliminated savings and much remaining wealth while the new assault on 'bourgeois trade' particularly affected the country's ethnic Chinese population of some 1.2 million. Approximately 130,000 people had fled from Vietnam in 1975 but this was soon dwarfed by the rate of refugees from the spring of 1978 onwards. It is thought that 675,000 people had left Vietnam by August 1979 including 250,000 ethnic Chinese who fled into China. About 60 per cent of the remainder who tried to escape by sea, and who became known as the 'boat people', were also ethnic Chinese. By July 1979 120,000 refugees had landed in Malaysia; 40,000 in Indonesia; 11,000 in the Philippines; 2100 in Singapore; 30,000 in Thailand; and 60,000 in Hong Kong. It is probable that at least 10 per cent of those attempting to escape were lost through drowning or piratical attack. The strain placed on the hosts by this mass emigration, which many suspected the Vietnamese government to be encouraging, was considerable. Malaysia took a hard line against 'illegal immigrants' while an international conference convened at Geneva in July 1979 extracted a promise from the Vietnamese to slow down the outward flow of refugees.

Khmer Rouge terror

Refugees were not confined to the population of Vietnam for in Cambodia, or Democratic Kampuchea as it was renamed by the Khmer Rouge in December 1975, the excesses of Pol Pot's Angka Loeu (Organization on High) far exceeded those in Vietnam. On the pretext of an inability to safeguard or feed the 2.5 million inhabitants of Phnom Penh when it fell, Khmer Rouge troops forced the entire population, including an estimated 200,000 inmates of the city's hospitals, to leave within eight days. In all some 3.5 million urban dwellers and 500,000 rural inhabitants were forcibly relocated in 'new villages' by the autumn of 1975 where malnutrition, hard labour and disease swiftly took their toll. A further enforced migration of 500,000 people from the south took place just before the harvest was due in the autumn of 1975.

In addition, the Khmer Rouge rejected re-education as a means of restruct-

Opposite far left: The destruction of the gates to the Presidential Palace in Saigon symbolized communist victory in the Vietnam War. Opposite left: Units of the NVA are greeted by children on the streets of Saigon. Right: Although the North Vietnamese authorities did not instigate a pogrom in the South, conditions were such that there was a steady exodus of refugees from Saigon and other urban areas of the former South Vietnam. Below: A boatload of refugees from the shores of Vietnam. The plight of the Vietnamese boat people caused widespread international concern.

uring society, and officials and soldiers of the Lon Nol government were systematically eliminated. The hatred generated towards 'intellectuals' was sufficient for it to be dangerous to be seen wearing glasses, while the indoctrination process turned children into informers against their parents. Figures vary but it is believed that as many as 1.4 million may have died from starvation, disease or execution by January 1977. Between 30,000 and 50,000 refugees had reached Thailand by April 1976 and by August 1979 it was calculated that 150,000 had fled to Thailand and 321,000 to Vietnam including 125,000 Khmers, 24,000 ethnic Chinese and 170,000 ethnic Vietnamese who had been a particular target for persecution. The situation became even more fluid in December 1978 when Vietnam invaded Kampuchea and ejected the Khmer Rouge, so that by the end of 1980 there was an estimated refugee population of 120,000 inside Thailand with some 500,000 assorted refugees and guerrillas along the Thai-Kampuchean frontier. By January 1982 the Thai policy of returning or resettling refugees had brought this figure down to 83,000 refugees in Thailand with a further 17,000 awaiting previously agreed resettlement in other countries. As well as the refugees from Vietnam and Cambodia, the communist government in Laos, although less severe than its neighbours, had also generated 250,000 refugees by August 1979, of whom half were from upland minorities who had previously supported the Americans.

The flight of ethnic Chinese from Vietnam and of ethnic Vietnamese from Kampuchea is in itself indicative of traditional antipathies that existed in Indochina throughout the years of nominal alliance against external powers such as France and the United States. Once this stimulus to cooperation was removed these older rivalries reasserted themselves, especially in terms of the relationship between Kampuchea and Vietnam

Below: Troops of the Vietnamese-sponsored Kampuchean Revolutionary Army move into the Cambodian forest in pursuit of the Khmer Rouge.

Above: Pathet Lao infantrymen surround a position occupied by Thai troops. Relations between the communist states of Laos and Cambodia and Thailand were poor and border clashes were common. Right: Vietnamese artillery shells a Khmer Rouge position. Well armed and trained, the Vietnamese armed forces were more than a match for the Khmer Rouge.

and between Vietnam and China. The Khmers, for example, regard the Vietnamese or 'yuons' as an inferior race. Vietnam had annexed part of the Khmer empire in the 18th century, principally the Mekong Delta and that part of Indochina known as Cochin-China during French rule. The French themselves had transferred other Khmer areas to Vietnam and there was also a long standing dispute over islands such as Phu Quoc in the Gulf of Thailand. More specifically the Khmer Rouge could interpret Vietnamese actions more recently as undermining their own efforts to seize power in Cambodia. Both the North Vietnamese acceptance of peace terms at Geneva in 1954 and at Paris in 1973 were seen as a desertion by the Khmer Rouge, the latter occasion enabling the United States to divert its bombers against them.

The Vietnamese had made extensive use of Cambodian territory during the war against the Americans but without offering the Khmer Rouge much reciprocal assistance, and they had been suspected of attempting to annex parts of Cambodia in 1967 and 1970. Both the Vietnamese promise to Prince Sihanouk in 1970 to respect Cambodian territorial integrity and the renunciation in 1978 of the ideas of Indochinese federation advocated by the Vietnamese communists since 1935 were regarded with suspicion, especially as the Vietnamese remained in possession after 1975 of areas within Cambodia from which they had operated during the war. At the same time, whatever Vietnam's intentions, it was possible, in turn, to interpret her eventual invasion of Kampuchea as a defensive reaction against Pol Pot's own apparent territorial aggrandizement which was disrupting the 'new economic zones' along the frontier.

Border clashes

Clashes occurred between Khmer Rouge and Vietnamese forces as early as 1974 but it was not until April 1977, following accusations by Pol Pot that the Vietnamese had attempted to instigate coups against him in the previous two years, that a major Khmer Rouge incursion took place. Attacking on a Vietnamese public holiday, Khmer Rouge forces advanced six miles (10 km) into Vietnam before withdrawal and a second attack on a subsequent public holiday in September 1977 achieved a penetration of some 95 miles (150 km). After some localized retaliatory incursions six Vietnamese divisions advanced into Kampuchea on 31 December 1977 and seized the vital Mekong river-crossing only 35 miles (56 km) from Phnom Penh. That this incursion was of a warning nature rather than the full-scale invasion claimed by the Khmer Rouge was indicated by the Vietnamese withdrawal and offer of a demilitarized zone along the frontier in February 1978. Having severed diplomatic relations with Vietnam in December, Pol Pot rejected this and further clashes occurred in April, June and July 1978. By the beginning of the dry season in the autumn of 1978 Vietnam had clearly resolved to act decisively against Pol Pot, many of the troops committed in June having remained inside Kampuchean territory. On 3 December 1978 a former Khmer Rouge commissar, Heng Samrin, was named head of a Vietnamese-sponsored Kampuchean National United Front for National Salvation (KNUFNS) and on 25 Decem-

Top: Soviet-built T55 tanks parade through the streets of Phnom Penh following the victory of the armed forces of the KNUFNS over the Khmer Rouge. Above: Cambodian premier and leader of the Khmer Rouge, Pol Pot. His savage attempts to reorganise Cambodia society helped lead to the deaths of millions of Cambodians.

ber some 12 Vietnamese divisions consisting of 120,000 Vietnamese troops invaded Kampuchea. The participation of 20,000 United Front troops enabled the Vietnamese to maintain the fiction that none of their own troops was involved. Pol Pot had anticipated the offensive and 60,000 Khmer Rouge troops were able to withdraw to previously prepared supply dumps in the jungles, Radio Phnom Penh announcing on 3 January 1979 that the Khmer Rouge would now wage a guerrilla campaign. It is possible that the Vietnamese hoped to avoid a prolonged conflict but their 'blitzkrieg' assault captured mostly empty cities and left them with long, exposed lines of communication. Phnom Penh fell on 7 January, the new People's Republic of Kampuchea being proclaimed on the following day. The casualties may have amounted to as many as 30,000 on each side.

Vietnamese rule extended

The fall of Kampuchea had immediate repercussions upon Sino-Vietnamese relations. Just as the conflict between Vietnam and Kampuchea had long antecedents so, too, had that between Vietnam and China. China had ruled Vietnam for over 1000 years until a successful Vietnamese revolt in AD 939 brought about a situation where the Vietnamese acknowledged the titular suzerainty of the Chinese but resisted any encroachments. The Vietnamese had defeated the Chinese forces on a number of occasions since. The French had then delineated the frontier in the late 19th century but the Vietnamese claimed that they had ceded Vietnamese territory to China. The long years of war in Indochina after 1945 saw North Vietnam obtaining support from both the Chinese and the Soviet Union but the relationship was never easy and the Chinese *rapprochement* with the United States and Nixon's visit to Peking in February 1972 while American aircraft were still bombing Vietnam led to a steady deterioration. This was exacerbated by territorial disputes in the Gulf of Tonkin and over the Paracel Islands (which China seized from South Vietnam in January 1974) and the Spratly Island group seized by the North Vietnamese from South Vietnam in April 1975.

The growing dependence of Vietnam upon the Soviet Union was also a major cause of conflict since the Chinese, like the Khmer Rouge, were suspicious of Vietnamese ambitions and the possible creation of a 'Cuba in Asia'. As far as China was concerned there was apparently little alternative to supporting Pol Pot, despite the international odium he attracted and despite the fact that he refused to accept Chinese advice. The flight of Vietnam's ethnic Chinese increased the tension, especially when the Vietnamese at first agreed to but then forestalled China's intention to evacuate her nationals by sea. The Chinese also believed that the Vietnamese were delaying the establishment of a Chinese consulate in Ho Chi Minh City. Thus when Vietnam joined Comecon (the international communist economic union) on 29 June 1978 the Chinese promptly cut off all economic aid (worth 30 million dollars annually), withdrew all their technicians, closed existing consulates and recalled their ambassador.

It is possible that the Chinese hoped such economic pressure, together with a build-up of troops along the frontier, would deter Vietnam from action in Kampuchea. In the event it pushed Vietnam closer to the Soviet Union, a treaty of peace and friendship being concluded between them on 3 November 1978. This in turn may have been a Vietnamese attempt to deter China from intervention but its immediate result was to speed Chinese normalization of relations with the United States. Some frontier clashes had already occurred and Vietnam later claimed there had been 2175 border incidents in the course of 1978. Thus when Vietnam invaded Kampuchea the Chinese senior vice-premier and deputy chairman, Teng Hsaio-P'ing,

Above: Vietnamese soldiers pose victoriously on a Chinese tank (a copy of the Soviet T55) knocked out in Cao Bang near the Vietnamese border with China.
Opposite far left: North Vietnamese troops prepare to fire a rocket launcher from a trench near the Chinese border.
Opposite left: Female Vietnamese soldiers guard captured Chinese troops near the battlefield of Cao Bang to the north-west of Hanoi.

made a point of talking of the need to teach Vietnam a 'lesson' during his tours of the United States and Japan in January 1979. On 17 February Chinese forces attacked at some 26 points along the 450-mile (725 km) length of the Sino-Vietnamese frontier.

A punitive action

It is likely that the Chinese had a secondary military aim of relieving some of the pressure on the Khmer Rouge but the primary motive for the invasion was political. Chinese action was to be punitive, indicating that she could inflict damage on Vietnam despite the latter's Soviet allies. Probably anticipating that the Soviets would not themselves initiate any military response, the invasion was also designed to sow doubt about the Soviets' worth as allies while demonstrating China's own willingness to support her friends. The Chinese thus announced that they would withdraw once Vietnam had been suitably 'punished'. However, the fighting did not go quite as the Chinese expected. Between 70,000 and 80,000 men were committed initially, the main thrust being directed towards important nodal centres at Lao Cai and Dong Dang. After regrouping and reinforcing to a strength of 200,000 the Chinese renewed their advance and took Lang Son after fierce fighting on 2 March 1979. The Chinese then withdrew in good order by 16 March, having laid waste four provincial capitals and inflicted considerable material damage. But the cost was heavy with the Chinese admitting to 20,000 casualties.

The Vietnamese probably suffered an equal number of losses but had held the Chinese with only 50,000 border troops and militia, preferring to hold back around Hanoi those front-line units not in Kampuchea. The Chinese may have underestimated the capabilities of the Vietnamese and their mass wave assaults with a force composed largely of infantry demonstrated both the obsolescence of much of the Chinese equipment and the army's lack of real combat experience since the Korean War. No aircraft were used by either side. The invasion did not weaken Vietnam's resolve and the Chinese were then requested to withdraw their remaining advisers from Vietnamese-dominated Laos.

Since the conclusion of the Sino-Vietnamese War the key to events in Indochina has remained the extent of Vietnamese ambitions. By 1979 Vietnam had 50,000 troops in Laos and some 200,000 in Kampuchea, her 600,000-strong army being the most powerful in Indochina. The treaties concluded between Vietnam and Laos in August 1977 and between Vietnam and Heng Samrin in February 1979 gave the Vietnamese effective control over their neighbours, while they were reported to be extending their influence in Burma by the autumn of 1980. The occupation of Kampuchea is, of course, also of immense significance to the Association of South East Asian Nations (ASEAN) and particularly Thailand. The Khmer Rouge themselves made incursions into Thailand in 1976 and 1977 and, since 1979, the Thais have been frequently accused by the Vietnamese of harbouring Khmer Rouge guerrillas. Serious clashes took place between Thai and Vietnamese forces in June and July 1980 and there were further large Vietnamese troop concentrations close to the Thai frontier during the 1980/81 and 1981/2 dry seasons (October to April) as the Vietnamese attempted to flush out the guerrillas. The Thai-Laotian frontier was closed as a result in February 1981. The situation is complicated by the presence alongside the remaining guerrillas of the Khmer Rouge (numbering between 35,000 and 50,000) of assorted non-communist guerrillas including between 3000 and 6000 men of the Khmer People's National Liberation Front (KPNLF) led by a former prime minister, Son Sann. A number of attempts have been made, principally by Prince Sihanouk, to form a united front against the Vietnamese, but so far with limited success. The Khmer Rouge itself replaced Pol Pot with Khieu Samphan in 1979 and abandoned its Marxist organization in December 1981 as a further attempt to win international recognition. The Vietnamese show no signs of quitting Kampuchea, having organized elections there in May 1981, but the Khmer Rouge still occupies the Kampuchean seat at the United Nations and, in May 1981, was still recognized by 84 states as opposed to the few clients of the Soviet Union who recognize Heng Samrin's Vietnamese-backed government.

A captured Chinese prisoner is paraded before the camera as part of a Vietnamese propaganda exercise. The success of the Chinese incursion into Vietnam in 1979 remains debatable, although, needless to say, both sides claimed victory.

Vietnam and South-east Asia

The danger to Thailand has forced ASEAN seriously to consider changing its original economic and social aims into some form of military alliance. In this regard Singapore has been noticeably more forceful than Malaysia and Indonesia although the Vietnamese failed to conclude bilateral treaties with individual members of the organization in 1978 and have so far failed fully to exploit the differences which clearly exist. ASEAN is mindful of the way in which Vietnam violated assurances of non-intervention in Kampuchea given in 1978 and of non-intervention in Thailand given in April 1980 and has sponsored United Nations motions condemning Vietnamese occupation of Kampuchea. It is, however, equally suspicious of China although the Chinese have dropped support for communist guerrillas operating in ASEAN states. The occupation of Kampuchea is also of continuing concern to the Chinese. Vietnamese dependence upon the Soviet Union has increased to the extent where the Soviets and their Comecon partners were subsidizing Vietnam to the tune of two million dollars a day in 1979. The Soviets have also increased their naval activity in the region, utilizing Cam Ranh Bay from May 1979 and Kompong Som from the summer of 1980. Tension on the Sino-Vietnamese frontier has also continued, China claiming 2000 border incidents in the 14 months to June 1980, and there were large-scale clashes in May and June 1981 on both the Sino-Vietnamese and Sino-Laotian frontiers. There is, however, relatively little China can do beyond supporting the weak and sporadic resistance movements inside Vietnam and giving aid to Meo guerrillas in Laos and the Khmer Rouge operating from Thailand.

Indochina is therefore still an area of conflict after 40 years in which warfare has solved very little and only added to the burden of misery of the population. And this state of affairs seems liable to continue for the foreseeable future.

Bibliography

R. Bonds (ed), *The Vietnam War* (Salamander, London, 1979)
P. Caputo, *A Rumor of War* (Macmillan, London, 1977)
M. Charlton and A. Moncrieff, *Many Reasons Why: The American Involvement in Vietnam* (London, 1978)
J. Davidson, *Indo-China, Signposts in the Storm* (Longman, Malaysia, 1979)
B. Fall, *Street Without Joy* (Harrisburg, 1966)
B. Fall, *Hell in a Very Small Place: The Siege of Dien Bien Phu* (London, 1966)
M. Herr, *Dispatches* (Picador, London, 1978)
S. T. Hosmer, K. Kellen and B. M. Jenkins, *The Fall of South Vietnam: Statements by Vietnamese Military and Civilian Leaders* (Rand, Santa Monica, 1978)
G. Lewy, *America in Vietnam* (New York, 1978)
E. O'Ballance, *The Indo-China War 1945-54* (London, 1964)
W. Shawcross, *Sideshow: Kissinger, Nixon and the Destruction of Cambodia* (Andre Deutsch, London, 1979)
F. Snepp, *Decent Interval: The American Debacle in Vietnam and the Fall of Saigon* (Random House, 1977)
Sir R. Thompson (ed), *War in Peace: An Analysis of Warfare since 1945* (Orbis, London, 1981)
Van Tien Dung, *Our Great Spring Victory* (Monthly Review Press, London, 1977)
D. Warner, *Certain Victory: How Hanoi Won the War* (Mission, Kansas, 1975)

Index

Figures in italics refer to the pictures